Dr Anna Gekoski has worked as and more recently has conducted forensic psychology. During her time as a national newspaper reporter she was the ghost-writer for the bestselling *Sara Payne: A Mother's Story*. She is also the author of *Murder by Numbers,* a psychological analysis of the childhoods of British serial killers. Anna has degrees in philosophy, criminology, and psychology, and a doctorate in forensic psychology.

Steve Broome is an experienced social and economic researcher and interviewer, having spent the past fifteen years conducting projects in areas such as mental health, substance misuse, unemployment, social inclusion, economic development, and crime. He now works as Director of Research at the Royal Society of Arts, the internationally renowned think-tank.

Anna and Steve are married to each other and live in Brighton with their dog, Mavis.

What's Normal Anyway?

Anna Gekoski and Steve Broome

Constable • London

Constable & Robinson Ltd
55–56 Russell Square
London WC1B 4HP
www.constablerobinson.com

First published in the UK by Constable,
an imprint of Constable & Robinson, 2014

ISBN 978-1-47210-518-9 (B-format paperback)
ISBN 978-1-47210-519-6 (ebook)

Printed and bound in the UK

1 3 5 7 9 10 8 6 4 2

This book is dedicated to our mums,
with love

Contents

Foreword

We all know someone who is affected by mental illness. It might be a family member, friend, neighbour, or colleague; now, or one day, it might be you. In fact, around a quarter of us will suffer from a mental health disorder every year, and up to half of us will do so at some point in our lives. Mental health problems are therefore remarkably common. So, as the title of this book asks: 'What's normal anyway?'

We both have some personal experience of mental illness. We know first-hand the variety of feelings and emotions that having a mental health condition can invoke: frustration, anger, loneliness, inadequacy, embarrassment, exhaustion, fear, desperation, and hopelessness. Having experimented with different types of therapies, medications, alternative treatments, and lifestyle changes, we also know how hard it can be to find something that helps. And we know the impact of mental ill health on every aspect of life: working, socialising, relationships, and families. Finally, we know just how difficult it can be to 'come out' and admit to having a problem because, despite how widespread it is, there is still a stigma attached to mental illness.

It was these personal experiences, and the lack of useful and accessible information relating to them, that sparked the idea for this book. We wanted to *write* the book that we ourselves wanted to *read*: one containing a series of frank, detailed, first-person accounts from others also suffering from mental health conditions. We wanted the comfort of knowing that we weren't alone, of hearing about other people's symptoms and their experiences of various treatments, and of being given the hope that we could recover. Thinking that other people in our position might want the same, we decided to combine our personal experiences of mental illness with our professional backgrounds in psychology and social research to produce this book.

We decided to ask 'celebrities', rather than 'ordinary' people, to share their stories with us because research shows that accounts of mental illness from famous people are particularly powerful. When a celebrity 'reveals' that they have been suffering from a mental health problem – in a media interview, autobiography, or on social media – the news frequently stimulates debate, and gets the public thinking and talking about mental illness. This is one of the reasons why celebrities are so often now used in awareness campaigns. A recent study by the mental health charity Mind found that one in three people changed their ideas about the sorts of people who can suffer from mental illness after hearing celebrities talking about their own experiences. Over a third said that such stories made them understand mental health disorders better, and one in five were inspired to start a conversation about mental health with someone close to them.

Not only do celebrity stories of mental illness improve general knowledge about mental health, challenge negative stereotypes, encourage compassion, and reduce stigma – they also directly encourage people to seek help. In fact, Mind found that one in five people who have sought help for a mental health problem have done so specifically because they heard a celebrity sharing their experience. These are,

therefore, the broad aims of this book, which, to our knowledge, is the first of its kind. In addition, we are raising money
for various mental health charities, by donating a percentage of
any royalties.

To make this book as useful and relevant to as many people
as possible, and to illustrate that mental illness does not discriminate, we approached a diverse range of British household
names. We are immensely grateful to those who enthusi-
astically and generously gave their time and support to this
project – not for sympathy or any kind of financial reward,
but often through a passionate desire to raise awareness about
mental health.

In the following chapters, an actor, footballer, television presenter, writer, Olympic medallist, two politicians, chat show
host, model, broadcaster and author all give their individual
accounts of the often taboo subject of mental illness. These ten
people suffer, or have suffered, from some of the most common types of mental health conditions, including depression,
bipolar disorder, anxiety, panic attacks, agoraphobia, obsessive
compulsive disorder, body dysmorphic disorder, anorexia, and
bulimia.

Their stories have both similarities and differences. Childhood
experiences, genetic influences, and stressful life events are
all talked about as possible triggers for mental illness. Views
on taking medication vary from outright refusal, to reluctant
acceptance, to welcome relief. Therapy is lifesaving for some,
a source of amusement (and bemusement) for others. Some
consider themselves recovered, others have learned to manage
or live with their conditions, and some view their experiences
not as 'disorders' at all but simply as part of who they are.
There is also discussion of the (often overlooked) positives
and potential benefits that going through such experiences
can bring.

These personal revelations are not traditionally 'ghost-written', but are written *as spoken* by the celebrities, through in-depth interviews with the authors. The accounts are presented in the subjects' own words: their use of language, patterns of speech, and experiences captured faithfully and presented, wherever possible, with minimal editing and polishing. This style has certain implications for the reader. The text does not always flow freely, but sometimes halts and stutters – as our voices naturally do – with some repetitions, hesitations, and conversational quirks left in rather than 'cleaned up'.

Some of these revelations come with a liberal sprinkling of hard language and strong opinion. The stories may also make difficult or distressing reading at times. They describe metaphorical dark tunnels, rooms, and clouds; hopelessness, helplessness, and despair; sensations of numbness or deadness; feelings of being overwhelmed, unable to cope, and out of control; of being panicked, edgy, jittery, and manic; of feeling suicidal and even attempting suicide. They certainly illustrate, as both Trisha Goddard and Stephanie Cole observe, that there's no glamour in mental illness.

As you read the following chapters some of their contents may resonate with you personally, or you may recognise some of the symptoms in someone you know. This may cause uneasy or upsetting feelings. If so, we suggest that you have a look at the factsheets at the end of this book, which give information about the various disorders described in the celebrities' accounts. You may also want to contact one of the organisations – whose details are provided – that can offer information, help, and support.

The stories in this book do not make comfortable reading, but mental illness is not a comfortable subject. If you want sanitised, easy to read, highly polished, heavily edited accounts, without a hint of profanity, this book may not be for you.

But if you want real accounts of mental illness – those with truth, power, passion, impact, and dignity – as well as stories of recovery, positivity, and hope – then please read on.

Anna Gekoski and Steve Broome, 2014

BILL ODDIE

Television presenter, writer, actor, musician, comedian, and birdwatcher

'If you want a bit of a consolation, most people who have bipolar, when they're on the manic side, they don't look at it as manic, they look at it as creative and energetic. You know, there is a good side to that, there actually is, because at least you're happy then. You might be about to do something really stupid but you're happy. And, let's be honest, it's not a boring illness. It's not: "Oh well, you've broken your leg, put a splint on it." It's horribly fascinating really, let's face it.'

Bill Oddie was born in 1941 in Rochdale and educated at Cambridge University, where he studied English Literature and was a member of the Footlights Club. In the 1960s he appeared on stage in the West End and on Broadway, wrote television scripts for *That Was The Week That Was*, was one of the stars of the BBC radio programme *Sorry, I'll Read That Again*, and released numerous records. Moving into the 1970s, Bill was one of the three creators, writers, and stars of the hugely popular television comedy show *The Goodies*, which ran from 1970 to 1982. He began his wildlife and birdwatching career in the 1980s and has since presented over twenty nature shows including *Springwatch* and *Autumnwatch*. After being diagnosed with clinical depression at the age of sixty, Bill had ten years of unsuccessful treatment before finally being re-diagnosed as having bipolar disorder after taking an overdose for the second time. After starting on lithium, his condition is now stable. He is the father of three daughters, Bonnie and Kate, from his first marriage to Jean Hart, and Rosie with his wife Laura. Bill and Laura live in London, where the interview for this chapter took place.

***

In a way I was a therapist's dream, I reckon. I remember thinking, the first session: 'This guy must think all his holidays have come at once.' First question every shrink asks you, the world over, is: 'Tell me about your mother.'

They all start off like that. And I remember saying:

'Well as soon as I do, you'll be like: Oh wow, I've got all the ingredients here.'

When I finished, he said: 'Your mother was in a mental home?'

'Yeah.'

'She wasn't there at all when you were a child? Not even when you were a baby?'

'No, that's right.'

'She attacked your father a couple of times?'

'Yeah, that's right.'

'Wooah, I'll have you for about seven or eight years, with all this to go through!'

So, yes, my mother was in a mental home for most of my childhood and I personally have no memory of living with her properly at all. I was born in Rochdale in Lancashire and the setup, in the little tiny house, was: my father, who was an accountant at the electricity board down the road, and his mother who was, I imagine, in her eighties or something . . . maybe a bit less than that when I was actually born, but certainly fairly elderly. But not decrepit in any way, she wasn't being looked after, it wasn't a care situation, it was more a blackmail situation I think! My dad had taken her on as she kind of had to go somewhere and his brother had actually refused to have my granny in the house.

I didn't know any of this until much later but, basically, my childhood take on it was: there's my dad, there's my granny, who lives with us, and that's the way it is. So my granny became *in loco parentis*, which wasn't entirely appropriate, I don't think. But my dad was really the person who brought me up and, even though he was working long hours, he was utterly and entirely scrupulous, dependable, and everything else. There was no way I could ever fault him. Sometimes he was a bit over-organisational or something, or over-ambitious on my behalf, but basically totally reliable. There was never any feeling of being a latchkey kid in Rochdale, which would have been easy casting really.

How much I knew about my mother at the time I don't know, as I've pieced some of it together since, via my mother's sister, who I got in touch with about ten years ago. But as a kid of that age you simply wouldn't . . . well, I didn't, for example, do the sort of things you might have thought I would do, like saying:

'Where's my mum by the way? Where did she go? I've noticed something: all these kids at school have this female that they . . .'

'That's the mother, dear boy.'

'Oh really? I don't think I've got one of those.'

Then a bit later I remember being told things like: 'Oh, your mother's gone to stay in a hotel for a while.' Or: 'She's gone to stay with a friend for a while.'

But there's a lot of things in life in general – and this is certainly one of them – where your take on it is different as the years go by. It varies, because it depends on what you know. And when I look back on it, what I knew about my mother at the time was pretty weird, but it didn't particularly strike me as that weird then. All I knew then, and this is the relevant thing really, was that she wasn't there. And I was used to her not being there and I suppose, relatively, not particularly troubled about it. In fact, I've since found out that she was first sectioned or whatever – they probably had some different name for it: 'carted-off' or something – in 1940-something.

My only consciousness, my only memory really, of my mother at home during that period – and it was still in Rochdale so I must have been only about five or six, cos we left and went to Birmingham after that – was coming back from school and there being broken crockery. I can visually kind of see it. You know, it looked as though there had been Greek dancing in the kitchen – it was everywhere – and then I realised there was blood on quite a lot of it. And my granny must have been there somewhere, but my dad wasn't. I was later told – I think by my granny, but I can't be sure – that my mother had been at the house and had attacked my dad, who was in hospital but was okay. Later, some time after he got home, he told me that my mother wasn't coming back. And I was relieved because at the time I was, and continue to be, quite scared of what I knew, because I knew that there was evidence of violence.

My mother was in the classic mental home, a big sort of pseudo-mansion, called Barnsley Hall. I went to see her once when I was a teenager and that was the only contact I had. I don't remember feeling upset particularly and I don't think I did right through that period; it was almost too unreal to feel depressed or upset by it. Because it really was . . . it was like a film set, with all the lighting and stuff, and long corridors, and every now and again there'd be some 'argh!' noise, or somebody crying, or somebody beating their head against the wall. And then you finally got down to these curtains and: 'This is your mother!' And she was just sitting there and she didn't recognise me . . . I stayed for, whatever, twenty minutes, I don't know, and there was no recognition. She just said: 'Television is dead bodies and cardboard.' (If only it were. It'd be more interesting than fucking chefs!) But, you know, I just . . . it didn't leave any impression except a visual one. The main impression it left was the fact that there wasn't an impression. That was the main thing. To actually come out and say: 'I'm sorry but what just happened there? Was that my mother? Are you sure?' Because it didn't mean a thing, she was a stranger.

As to what was wrong with her, all I'd ever been told – back in the old days, back in the '40s and '50s – was that she had: 'Trouble with her nerves, she has trouble with her nerves.' And I never knew what that meant. Did it mean: 'Oooh, you're nervous all the time'? But it was always that – 'trouble with her nerves' – it just filled anything in. Other than her 'nerves', the only other so-called retrospective diagnosis I had around that time was when I'd left university and she'd just been taken out of the hospital by, I think, her mother. And I'd rung up the doctor and asked what exactly was wrong with my mother because nobody had said anything. And he said: 'Oh, she was schizophrenic.' Yes, schizophrenic, and could be violent and dangerous and that sort of thing. And obviously, in her case, she *was* prone . . . I know because of the crockery incident that there was violence involved.

Years later though, in 2003, I got another perspective on it when I was doing the telly series *Who Do You Think You Are?* and I met a couple of nurses who had treated my mother at Barnsley Hall, who were now in their late eighties, nineties. And how the hell they were so clear I don't know, because they said:

'Oh yes, we remember your mother, she was so jolly.'

'Eh?'

'Yes, yes, she was always singing and playing the piano.'

'What? I had no idea she played the piano.'

'Yes, she did.'

So at the end of that I said: 'What do you think was wrong with her?'

And one of the ladies said: 'Oh, I think she had what we would now call bipolar.'

And, well, you know ... definitions. Having found out as much as I can over these last ten years – that's relevant to myself, not just from curiosity – diagnoses change, words change, don't they? So it's very difficult to know exactly what went on, but from what I've read and heard since it fits bipolar better than schizophrenia really. Looking back on it now I think, yes, my mother did have bipolar disorder.

★★★

What hadn't happened . . . I certainly hadn't gone through life thinking my mother had a very bad problem. I certainly hadn't gone through my life, at all, thinking: 'I wonder if this will clobber me in any way or other?' But I have to say – although I wouldn't necessarily blame anyone – that looking back now you'd think that some doctor or somebody might have said: 'Your mother did what? She was where? Ah. Oh. Well, we'd better keep an eye on you then.' But the suggestion that there was some flaw there that might have been passed on genetically never cropped up. So I was not aware, and I don't think anyone else was aware on my behalf, as it were, that I had any problem until about 2000, very late on, when I was about sixty. It wasn't 'til I had what one would have called in the old days a 'nervous breakdown', which in fact was a heavy dose of clinical depression (or at least that was certainly what the doctor said then) that I actually thought: 'There's something wrong with me here.'

I'm aware, thinking back – which is the best I can do in a sense – of a couple of little incidents which suggested that there was a bit of wiring starting to get loose in the lead up to the breakdown. Because, you know, it wasn't crazy, it was, sort of, disorientation. One time I was doing a voice-over in the morning, then I had to go somewhere else for a meeting, and then go back again. And I couldn't remember having done the voice-over. And the guy said: 'You did that this morning', and I said: 'No, I didn't', and he had to play it back to prove it to me. And I was, you know: 'Oh fuck, what happened there then? Is it memory? Is it just something switching off?' And I had a couple of those. I think the other one was when I had to drive down to Newquay to give a talk and, again, I was suddenly: 'Have I done the first half?' It was almost like you had concussion or something like that.

Something similar also happened to me when I was in Costa Rica and I was tipped overboard out of a white water raft type thing. And I was wearing a helmet and I didn't hit my head or anything – as far as I know – but I actually lost about an hour or so. I remember being in the boat, being in the water, and reaching up and somebody grabbing hold of me. Then the next thing I knew I was sitting in the front of the boat, paddling along quite happily, and the producer who was with me said:

'Are you okay?'

And I said: 'I don't think I am actually. Where am I?'

'You're in Costa Rica.'

'Am I? Are you sure?'

Eventually the only thing that got me round to accepting this was when we stopped and went to this little café by the river and I said: 'I'm just going to go for a walk for a few minutes.' So I got my binoculars and wandered round and started seeing toucans and things. And I thought: 'Ahh! This is not the Heath . . . you're in Kansas now!' So that's what brought it back. So I had quite a few little fades in and out of focus for a while.

Then . . . I don't remember the exact chronology of this . . . well, you don't write it all down do you? So it's fairly muddy in a way. But I do remember that first breakdown all too clearly. You know, all those clichés like: 'You don't know what it's like until you've had it', came flooding in. And I couldn't believe it, I just could not believe it, and anybody who's had the full whack, I'm sure, would say that. It's not a matter of just: 'I'm not feeling too good' or 'I've lost a bit of enthusiasm.' It's cut off, cut off, you've been unplugged. I was just absolutely inert, I just really couldn't move. I'd just lie on this couch day after day basically. You really are catatonic: you won't do anything, you can't do anything, you really are down and out. And it was a terrible shock obviously.

And I went to the GP and I couldn't talk. Laura, my wife, went with me and I was just sitting staring at the floor and I couldn't put two words together. I'd just turned into some sort of awful vegetable. And he said: 'You've obviously got clinical depression and it looks as bad as I've seen.' They were the words the doctor used. But at least we knew then, I suppose, that there was some sort of label on there, which was that I was prone to clinical depression, which was the first time that words like that had been anything to do with me as a patient. I don't recall anything else very much about the visit except some pills, some standard antidepressants or whatever, SSRIs or something. And there was a bit of a therapy attempt, which, of course, at that point, was with an NHS therapist. And it was fine, I didn't mind going, I didn't mind chatting, but I didn't find it . . . I don't know if I found it particularly helpful. Undoubtedly the biggest 'flaw', in inverted commas, was the fact that you'd be very lucky if you went once every ten days, or two weeks, and they would say: 'Look, I'd love to be able to see you every couple of days but I can't, it's not going to happen.'

The other thing you soon learn is that certain things are going to be part of your life. The ideas and the jargon – 'you've got this, you've got that' – was one of them. Although bipolar, manic depression, didn't enter into it at that point, it was never mentioned then, or if it was . . . actually there was one time . . . it was suggested once, in the early days, by a consultant on the NHS. I remember one session with her, very early on, when she said something like: 'We ought to look at the bipolar thing as well, let's have a think about that.' But, if you like, I almost dissuaded her because my concept of manic depression, as most people's concept of manic depression would be, was: you have your terrible downs, and these are balanced by ups that are so extreme that you think you can do all sorts of things you can't do, etc. And, you know . . . it's dangerously manic.

And I had an example because we knew some people up the road and the guy had been certified as bipolar. And his manic phases, of which I'd seen one or two, had been classically extreme. It was the early days of the Internet so he'd been on there buying all sorts of crap – he'd bought a house somewhere up in Scotland – and at one point he left his wife and was then seen advertising on the Internet or something. And God knows what. But he did the lot. And it didn't take you two seconds to say: 'Uh-oh, he's crazy.' And then the rest of the time he'd be in bed and not move – and I'd recognise that bit – and in between times there might be a bit that's okay. So that was my example of bipolar.

So when the consultant said: 'So how are you doing now then?'

And I said: 'I feel really good actually.' And I did, I felt really good at that point.

And she said: 'Not *too* good, I hope?'

And I said: 'Erm . . . oh, bipolar you mean? No, I'm not too good. Manic is not . . . like that.'

And I instanced this friend of mine and said: 'I know what happens to people, they jump off buildings and think they can fly and that sort of thing.' So they have this image of being real crazy.

And I said: 'I'm not that. I am not that.'

So therefore, during the next ten years, I had expunged the idea of manic depression because I had a certain idea of it and – aside from this woman – nobody else had taken it at all seriously either.

Aside from the jargon, the therapy, the pills, the next thing that becomes a part of your life is the question: 'Are you going to need to go into a hospital at some point or another?' Which I did. I went to the Priory first – the North London Priory – and everything about the two or three hours that I spent there was awful, from the minute I drove through the gates and along the path, through the bloody great gardens. You know, it looks like a stately home or something and it immediately reminded me of where my mother had been – instantly – which didn't help. And then it just gave me the creeps. I was registered or something and left in this room, this big room, and Laura stayed with me, and it was: 'Somebody will be back soon.' And I really freaked out. I was cowering in a corner, saying: 'Please, please don't leave me here, don't leave me here,' and she was saying: 'We've got to do this.'

Nobody turned up for about two hours and when they did they said:

'Oh, there's a phone call for you.'

And I said: 'But nobody knows I'm here.'

And they said: 'Oh, it's a newspaper.'

And I said: 'You've got to be bloody joking, I've only been here a couple of hours and somebody in this place has leaked that fact to the papers.'

You know, unbelievable. It happens, but I did think that was a bit quick. So I just couldn't . . . there was no way . . . I had to get out of that place. So I ended up in another hospital in town. (It's a private one too, but that's another issue, I'll come back to that.) And to cut a long story short I had to go in there about three times during a ten-year period.

***

Then there was the therapy − both in and out of hospital − which, among other things, set me off knowing what shrinks did. And, like I said before, it's such classic stuff: that you lacked mother love, that you lacked attention, motherly attention and support, and the person who was supposed to be looking after you ran away. You could . . . it's like a comedy sketch of what the basic things are that are going to bring you down, and that's a classic one obviously. The possibility of a genetic thing was interesting because that didn't get mentioned much, the therapist immediately homed in on the deprivation of mother love. I mean . . . I don't know whether it's true or not true, whether it's valid or not valid, whether it's the reason or just one reason, I haven't a clue. But he's going to go through every aspect of that.

It's a whole other subject this therapy stuff. And you don't have to be in a private hospital to get the therapy but I've seen these things going on in them. It borders on the comic, it borders on the grotesquely amusing, I'm afraid. I don't wanna say it doesn't work but they stick the word therapy on anything, you know:

'So, are you going to art therapy today?'

'Yes.'

'Are you going to dance therapy later?'

'Yes.'

'Have you got social therapy?'

'What's that?'

'Well, it's playing dominoes actually.'

'Right.'

'We're going to do gardening therapy!'

'We're going to do birdwatching therapy!'

'We're going to be doing sitting-and-watching-David-Attenborough-therapy!'

'Something-else therapy . . . blah-blah therapy.'

They're all given a name. What's the fashionable one at the moment? Oh God, that self-orientated thing, erm, it is aware-ness? Mindfulness, that's the one. You're supposed to go to that therapy. Also music therapy, that was a good one, a lot of people seemed to like that. Which is basically about the same as at a mother-and-toddler club, basically the same as at infant school. They leave a pile of percussion instruments – I could have lent them some – and there's usually a teacher who pretends to play the piano, but can't really, and everyone's meant to go like that and sort of make a noise and let it all out and that sort of thing. And the same when you do your art therapy, you paint something and then somebody will interpret it: 'Mmm, yeah, this is you gloomy, a big cloud, oh dear, it's tough isn't it?' 'No, it's actually raining.' I'm loath to knock them because I know a lot of people seem to like them but, as you've gathered, I just got more and more cynical about those sort of things and I didn't find them any use whatsoever. Aside from, occasionally, the naughty use of finding a couple of kindred souls, giggling most of the way through.

And, of course, looming over them all is cognitive behavioural therapy. Well, I don't know, I've been to quite a few of those and I can honestly say, I'm afraid for me – and I don't want to knock it – that I don't know what it's about, I really don't. I wish I didn't feel like this, it's one of the reasons I've been a bit cautious of talking about things, but every time somebody stands up there and does a pie chart and starts writing things on it I . . . I just *cannot* get with it at all. If you were to believe the papers – particularly the *Daily Mail* – there will be somebody there saying: 'CBT saved my life', or whatever, so I've got to accept that it does. But I also . . . I also can't help thinking: 'Well, yes, but it's very cheap for the NHS or whoever too.' It's a pretty basic thing, particularly if it's group therapy. But then again, to some people the group is important, I've seen it work. You know, I've been to so many of these sessions at the hospitals, there's always somebody nagging you. And you go along and sometimes it's just like a good chat with a bunch of people and if you get the right group it can be very interesting.

I don't know . . . the trouble is you always feel you shouldn't criticise something if you can't come up with something better and I can see that. But I think if you're of a certain mind and have a certain take – and you have a facetious sort of streak as I tend to do – then you've had it once you start giggling and you're given the nuts to hold or something like that. You think:

'Oh God almighty, I can't do this!'

And it's: 'How interesting, what are you feeling now?'

We had an American lady as well, which seemed strangely appropriate:

'What do you feel now?'

'Um, I'm a bit bored really.'

'Interesting, interesting.' That was her catch phrase.

There were two other guys at the back and we were like naughty pupils:

'Oh, that's interesting, interesting.'

Oh God. You know, I just want to write something there, I think there's a sitcom or something in it.

***

How did it affect my work? Luckily, during that stage – because this coincides mainly with my wildlife career – it didn't affect me very much professionally, because I was very fortunate that one of the producers I worked for was very sensitive about the problem. I think she had probably had problems herself at some point or certainly knew people who had. And I remember her very well. A couple of things. One, when we had finished the series we were working on she sent me a card, because she knew I wasn't in very good shape, saying: 'Don't worry about it, the job is still here, if we have to delay the next series it doesn't matter, it's okay.'

And another one was, I was supposed to go to Kenya and do some Christmas special and I could feel myself getting really edgy about it. And, again, she stepped in and said: 'Do you really wanna go?'

And I said: 'Ahh, I dunno.'

And she said: 'Look, I don't think you should because you'll be stuck out there and you won't have proper medical attention immediately. It hasn't really been sorted out properly and it doesn't matter.'

And a lot of people will say: 'Go ahead and test yourself!' But I can honestly say – and this is general advice in life – if you don't really wanna do it, just don't do it, and you'll be amazed at how much better you'll feel. You know: 'I don't have to go and do that! Great!' Anyway, so there was that degree of sympathy, which was so important at the time. God yes, it was a relief. But I can see exactly why there are jobs where people think: 'I mustn't let them know, I mustn't let them know.' It just depends on the attitudes of who you're working for and, in this particular case, at that particular time, I had sympathy from that one producer.

There was only one time when I ever really broke down in public, which was when I was supposed to give a talk to these people who worked on oil rigs . . . that's the only time I really had to stop, you know? But if we're looking for the brighter side of things, it showed that you only have to be in a room with half a dozen people and you find that at least a couple of them will have had this sort of experience, because the organiser of the event said:

'Do you have problems with depression?'

'Yeah.'

And he said: 'I thought so, I recognised that instantly. Don't worry about it, it's okay, it doesn't matter. It's only a bunch of people who probably don't know what you're talking about anyway!'

And that was partially true because, although I'd been on television all year, I had a room full of people working on the oil rigs all year! And I said: 'Has anybody seen *Springwatch*? . . . No?' Oh, Christ.

The irony, I suppose, of my journey – for want of a better, less pretentious, word – is that what has got me into trouble is not depression. It wasn't the depressive side, it was the manic side. Although I didn't know it was a manic side then, I didn't know I had a manic side. And that, I think, is not a very good comment on some of the people who were supposed to have been treating me or noticing that. The word bipolar – manic depressive – had not been applied to me or suggested to me, either by anybody else or myself, for years and years, since that NHS consultant I saw very early on. And, like I said, I dismissed it because of the exaggerated image of manic depression, which sounds like you're a total lost cause.

But leading up to 2009 I was behaving in a way which was more extreme. It wasn't outrageous frankly, but it was more extreme, looking back. It was all very, very work related. In the manic phase it was all to do with me having a perhaps inflated – you see I won't even accept it now: *perhaps* – inflated sense of knowing best, constantly saying: 'You don't understand.' You know, I basically lost it with a couple of producer/directors, where I said: 'For Christ sake, can't you concentrate, can't you see that this is meant to be like this?' Or: 'Will you please follow *my* script not yours.' And without going into gory details or non-gory details there were reasons behind all this. I wouldn't say that any of it was completely illogical, although there are probably people who would refute that and say it was illogical and I wasn't justified in saying I knew better. Was it divorced from reality? That's a good way of putting it. No, it wasn't divorced from reality and I don't remember anything that completely was, although people have told me that I said things or made statements which I can't really remember. But no, no, it definitely wasn't cardboard and dead bodies, it was kind of truth-game type stuff, you know? I was going to go in and tell you exactly what I thought of you and what's going on.

Then at the start of 2009, I got very, very depressed again, spending days in bed sleeping or staring at the walls. And the last four years have been the biggest drama one way or t'other: I ended up hospitalised for a fair chunk of time, I took overdoses twice, which is not a very bright thing to do, and tried to smuggle a blade of some sort into the hospital. All that kind of thing. At first I went back to the private hospital but, for a start, I really couldn't afford to be there, in a financial sense. It just wracked up half my bloody pension that I could have given to my kids. Also, as time went on, Laura was saying: 'Honestly, I know you don't think you were kind of over the top in that period last year, but I think you were, and can we talk about the bipolar situation?' But the consultant, the private consultant, seemed to sort of ignore it: 'No, let's just try a little bit more of this and a little bit more of that.' And Laura was getting totally frustrated: 'We can't go on like this, it's going to bankrupt us, you're not getting any better.'

And she, Laura, was very much building up a general antipathy towards the hospital. Possibly over the top, but I can see what she meant. Laura felt so strongly about it that I found myself going with her and getting this feeling, if you're really being critical, that at the private hospital they were keeping you there as long as possible to get as much money as they could out of you. Yep. Laura definitely feels that; she actually wrote to the consultant. And naturally got a rebuke, a rebuttal, but on the other hand it wasn't a terribly sympathetic one, it wasn't: 'I can understand you feeling like this, but . . .'. It was: 'Of course I wouldn't, anyway I must go, I've got another patient.' So, to cut a reasonably long story short, Laura eventually virtually refused to have anything more to do with the private hospital and I'm glad she did.

Anyway, after the second of the overdoses I got whisked off by the Camden emergency team . . . I've forgotten what they're called . . . the crisis centre, that's right. I was taken off, still totally groggy and everything, and plonked in the crisis house, which is fortunately not too far away. And it's all NHS stuff and they were wonderful, it's a really great facility. And while in there – I was in there about ten days, maybe nearly two weeks – one of the doctors who came in said: 'You're quite clearly bipolar.' I honestly think it was almost as simple as them saying: 'You've had ten years where you've been having depressions and it hasn't got any better' – and probably myself and Laura saying there was this period which, looking at it more critically, could be defined as having a manic episode – 'so let's assume that it is bipolar.'

Which type of bipolar disorder did they diagnose? They didn't do it, I did it. And this is quite an important specific point. You know, I haven't just accepted this all the time, I've read quite a bit. With the bipolar thing it was reading a book called *Bipolar Disorder – The Ultimate Guide*, written by two ladies, Sarah Owen and Amanda Saunders, and it's really good, with case histories and people explaining things. And the revolutionary moment for me was when somebody was explaining and they said: 'I was continuing with my work, and I was working very well, and I felt my work was getting better and better, and then I found myself getting irritable with other people and getting resentful of the fact that they couldn't keep up with me. And I'd get argumentative and dictatorial and say: "What's the matter with you? I can do this, why can't you do it?"' And my mind kept going: 'Tick, tick, tick', and I thought: 'Fuck, that is me, that really is me.'

Because when I look back to the autumn of the previous year – in context, I was working on *Autumnwatch* at the time

– I was getting increasingly annoyed with people at work. It was a period where I did have rows with several people and the reason was always that I couldn't see why they couldn't keep up, or they didn't understand, or they weren't doing their job properly. And to my mind I was justified as well: 'You're doing a fucking awful job, aren't you?' And it got to the point one day when, for whatever reason, I had an art easel, and I didn't throw it at anybody but I did hurl it on the floor and said: 'You're not even bloody trying are you?' And when I read that statement in the book, I tell you, it just fitted me exactly. I was thinking: 'Look, that's perfectly classic bipolar', but I'd never thought of that as bipolar. I can't remember what sort it is – whether it's A, B or nearly C, or whatever – but it's not the top one, whatever that is. Bipolar I? That's right, bipolar I is: 'Whoa, you're in trouble!' Is it II the lower one? Yeah, it well comes within that. So, to summarise that: it needn't be crazy behaviour, in my case it was over-confidence, over-cocky, that sort of thing.

And then I started thinking: 'Go back through your life.' And something else that another producer had said came back to me:

'You do frighten people a bit in the office.' (Not the sitcom. With Ricky Gervais.)

He said: 'You do frighten them sometimes.'

And I said: 'What?!'

And he said: 'Yes.'

And I said: 'How?'

And he said: 'Well, you're just very abrasive and they feel that they can't do their job properly or they haven't done their job properly.'

And I said: 'I hear what you're saying and I know what you mean, because what happens is, in my head, I get so absorbed in what we're doing in the show that I just want everybody to be there and get it done and I'm sure it comes over the wrong way sometimes.'

Then, thinking back even further, I remembered – God knows when, '70s or '80s or something like that – somebody else saying a similar thing. I was told: 'There are actually a few people who don't want to work with you, because you're too abrasive, demanding.' And I remember one or two other occasions from years ago. So the whole thing has made me look back as much as I can on my life and think: 'When I had a burst of something, could that have been of a bipolar nature?' And it's made me think: 'Hmm, well, maybe I did have this reputation and maybe that's why.' Because I had a manic edge which made people uncomfortable or something. But I never believed it, I thought I was easy. It's terrible, it's terrible. That's one of the things that's genuinely surprised me in my life, when I was told that people were scared of me. I thought: 'What?! It can't be.' I thought I was my charming self, but there you go.

But one of the things that's now become clear – that's relevant – is how varied something can be: that you can have a harsh version or not as harsh a version. And it's true of other things: if you've got a physical ailment sometimes you have a bad attack and sometimes it's not such a bad attack, and so on and so forth. There are variations and that's one of the things that perhaps needs to be recognised more by the medical profession in general. You know: 'I am prone to melancholy' is not the same as: 'I'm having a complete fucking breakdown.' And being manic is like that. It doesn't have to be the extremes of behaviour that I witnessed with the guy I knew up the road. If somebody had explained to me ten years ago that there is a disorder where you're very confident and then you're miserable, I might then have put the two together and thought: 'Okay, yes, I'll accept that.'

When I now describe bipolar to people who don't know about it – I do this at my granddaughter's school – I say:

'With bipolar, one minute you're really happy and doing lots of things and have lots of energy, and then on the other side you feel totally miserable and it's dreadful.'

And then you get onto the difficult bit. You say:

'Now, sometimes, you can be very unhappy, and you may be suicidal' – and let's face it, it's a cause of a lot of suicides – 'and on the other hand when you're up and happy and energetic, you might do some very good things as well as some very stupid things.'

And if you want a bit of a consolation, most people who have bipolar, when they're on the manic side, they don't look at it as manic, they look at it as creative and energetic. You know, there is a good side to that, there actually is, because at least you're happy then. You might be about to do something really stupid but you're happy. And, let's be honest, it's not a boring illness. It's not: 'Oh well, you've broken your leg, put a splint on it.' It's horribly fascinating really, let's face it.

★★★

Anyway, go on with your questions if you want or I'll just burble on. Actually, there's one thing I really want to say. Shall I just get it out the way? This concerns lithium. (Everybody thinks batteries first: you take batteries, they keep you going, recharge you.) Over the years I'd built up a picture that it was this drug that you really shouldn't risk, that it was the last resort, you really shouldn't take it – 'Oh God!' – you know? Why, particularly, nobody said, but it was: 'No, no, no, no.' I also knew this guy who was bipolar who refused to be on lithium. And I'm thinking: 'Well, he's had a lifetime refusing to take it, so there must be a reason for that.' So you get fed these

things from other people and I had this image that was really
bad. But then, funnily enough, things seemed to turn around,
coincidentally almost, because I mentioned it to my ex-wife,
who I get on very well with. So I was telling her about this,
and she said:

'Oh yeah, a friend of mine's been on lithium most of his
life.'

And I said: 'Really? Any problems?'

And she said: 'No, he's got other problems, but not with
that.'

And this happened with two or three people and it was:

'Oh, are they? But I thought it was really dangerous or
something.'

So Laura and I both, I think, said to the doctor: 'Why aren't
you trying lithium?' Because we'd come to the same conclusion having talked to a few people. But it was sort of dismissed
a bit: 'Oh, no, no, no, there's better things than that now,
you shouldn't take that, it's very old-fashioned.' You get this
sort of thing. But anyway, the point is, I thought: 'Sod it, I'm
going to try this.' And I'm not kidding, just a week or so after
I'd taken an overdose, I start me lithium and within a week
or ten days I'm really beginning to notice a difference. After
two weeks . . . this is ridiculous . . . I'm really getting better.
My kids were ringing up one another and saying: 'He's back!'
And it was just before Christmas, which was even better, and
I've been on it since and I . . . I don't understand what all the
fuss is about.

But then you go and see your doctor again and you say:
'Look, I've taken lithium and I'm so much better, I can't tell
you.' And it's: 'Ah well, yeah, well, it does work for some
people' – that's what they always say – 'but not for everyone,
it doesn't work for everyone, you're very lucky.' Yeah, okay,
good. So if anybody asks me all I can say is: 'Look, yes, I'm

probably lucky in that it seemed to work for me.' It hasn't worn off, it hasn't gone up and down or anything like that. Side effects? Very few. I think early on there were a couple of side effect things which were pretty bloody standard ones: more diarrhoea than you'd like for a day or two, and then a bit of a dry throat, one or two like that. And I could say that sexually it doesn't do a lot for you but, having said that, that might not be the lithium anyway, because I've been on antidepressants so long. I still take those too. I take everything at the moment.

I mean, it's an interesting journey in a way, when you start comparing with other people, you know, because I don't mind taking pills, but it's amazing how many people do. And I just find that kind of, a bit sort of . . . a bit daft in some ways. It just doesn't make sense to me to actually have a hang-up about taking pills, I don't know why people do. And coming off them too: why do so many people do that when they're working? I wouldn't risk coming off the lithium, I actually wouldn't risk it now. Although what I do suspect is that I'm still taking pills left over from the old regime – i.e. a couple of antidepressants – which are doing nothing. On the other hand they might be, so why risk it? I've got four blood pressure pills, so . . .

★★★

I can honestly say I feel absolutely fine now, I don't feel any-thing but fine. The biggest legacy is reminders of things, I find. I'll be walking down the street in a certain place and it'll be near where I used to go for therapy and I'll just go: 'Ah shit. Christ.' I mean it's not terribly upsetting but it triggers off a resentment where you go: 'Ah, two bloody years or, in the case of therapy, six bloody years traipsing backwards and forwards.' You know, add all that up, money-wise as well. I do feel resentful of the misdiagnosis. Yeah, I do, I do. I'm afraid I find myself resenting the fact that it buggered up about three or four years, that I lost a long period of time really. I can see nine-tenths of the time that it's the same old reasons – that people don't have long enough with you so don't have time to explore things properly perhaps, and it is complicated – but there are some things that GPs could do better.

A couple of years ago when I had got through all this, and I was certainly *compos mentis*, I did about three open days at some conference for GPs about mental health and how they can improve in their treatment of it. (Quite a bit is the answer.) So you've got a room full of a couple of hundred GPs and I sort of went through the whole story. A lot of it was really fresh in my mind and I really wanted to make these points, you know? One of the main points, from a GP's point of view, was to try to involve anybody else in the family. Because obviously, a very simple rule is: if you've got bipolar, on some days you're going to feel happy, you feel up, you feel confident. Are you going to go to the doctor then? No, of course not, you think you're fine. They only ever see you when you're miserable. But your wife or your children, or somebody else – a work mate – are more likely probably to think: 'You think you're really up there but I'm telling you, you're acting strange actually.' So I said: 'Try and take more notice, or even invite any notice, from parents or whatever.' Because they're going to see a lot more of it than the GP, who'll only ever see you miserable – 'Oh, you're depressed' – or see you saying there's nothing wrong.

And another, simply enough, was: 'I plead with you, if one of your patients comes to you and says they are clinically depressed, then ask about the other side of things. Just consider bipolar.' Because it's complicated, you know? If you suffer from depression it's awful but it's a bit more straightforward in a weird sort of way. But something that came out when we did those talks was that quite a few of the GPs said: 'I couldn't get the other people in my practice to come along today and, believe you me, there are plenty of GPs' – and this is them talking – 'who pretend it doesn't exist.' It's a very alarming statement. One said: 'Yeah, I'm afraid there's quite a few who just do the: "Oh yeah, sure, take this dear."' Which is a horrible idea. In attitude terms it's obviously unforgivable if a GP doesn't give full credence to mental health matters. Dreadful.

As for a message to other sufferers, the first thing you have to say, and everybody does say it fortunately, but get it through and make it real, is: 'You are not alone and it *will* make you feel better to talk to other people who have had other problems.' Obviously I'm very aware of this process of people being embarrassed or whatever, or not wanting other people to know . . . what was the phrase you used? The stigma of it and that sort of thing. But I think the stigma is far more in the mind of the sufferer than in other people's minds and if you can realise that then you won't feel as bad as you did about it. Because of that statistic – one in four – chances are you're going to get sympathy, in just the same way as if you've broken a leg or something like that. I think people are sympathetic about it because, let's face it, they know what it's like, or they know somebody else. So I think that it's just like . . . yes, an internal stigma . . . you don't want to be like this, you don't want to be in that situation, so it's you who doesn't want to know about it really.

This question of stigma is interesting in a way, because it's a question that should be put to people who don't have the problem, asking *them*: 'What would you think about somebody you know who, in this case, has bipolar?' Because there are various reactions available aren't there? One would be: 'Er, who hasn't? Very fashionable these days.' And let's face it, there is some danger of that, there is a little bit of danger of that. I talked to somebody the other day at one of these mental health groups and said: 'Are you sure there isn't a bit of a danger here of always having celebrity sufferers?' And I know it's to get the publicity and all that sort of thing but I wouldn't blame a punter – a normal member of the public who's got these problems and then hears Ruby, or Stephen, or me, or one or two others – for saying: 'Oh for fuck sake, show business isn't it?' I really wouldn't blame them at all for saying: 'Well it's easy for you mate, you're a bleeding millionaire.' You know: 'That's him, not me.'

And in terms of the differences between how celebs and normal people are treated, I would say that the celebrity is certainly not going to be excluded or pilloried and, if anything, I would imagine gains a bit in a sense, as you become interesting. And in a funny sort of way you get forgiven because you're an artist or something: you can be a bit mad and that's alright. Look at any amount of entertainers, writers, poets, musicians – it's always argued that people in history have been bipolar in one way or t'other. That's the artistic temperament. It's almost obligatory really:

'I've got an ambition to be a writer.'

'Are you bipolar?'

'No.'

'Well, forget it.'

So I think there is a bit of a danger with it becoming the celebs' illness. On the other hand, the organisations and people I've spoken to tend to say: 'No, we relate to the fact that somebody in the public eye is prepared to talk about it and say they have that trouble too.' And if that makes them feel less sensitive about it, or whatever, then good.

ALICIA DOUVALL

Former model

'To me, being body dysmorphic is like being imprisoned by your own mind because you're locked into the most powerful thing in the world, which is your own self. And you know, there's no answer, there's no escape from it . . . It's very hard to have a normal life in any shape or form: you can't have a proper relationship, you can't believe anyone who says you're beautiful or good looking, you can't walk down the street or be in crowded places because you think everyone's going to be looking, and pointing, and laughing at you. You're just never happy with yourself.'

Born Sarah Howes in Horsham, West Sussex, in 1979, Alicia Douvall became a glamour model while still a teenager, regularly appearing on Page 3 and *Playboy TV*. She has taken part in several reality TV shows, including *Celebrity Love Island* and *Celebrity Rehab*, and is the subject of three television documentaries: *Rehab: Alicia Douvall*, *Glamour Models, Mum & Me*, and *Glamour Model Mum, Baby & Me*. Alicia began to suffer from anorexia and bulimia as a teenager and later with body dysmorphic disorder (BDD), which has led to her having more than 350 surgical and cosmetic procedures. Having attended a rehabilitation clinic in the US three times, she has now started her own organic skincare company, Douvall's. Alicia lives in London with her two daughters, Georgia and Papaya.

★★★

My dad was a local Conservative councillor, a self-made millionaire, and just a very, very strict person. It felt like we all lived in fear. In what way? Gosh, it's awful, I don't even know where to start. Well, for instance, most people would look forward to a holiday, or a birthday, or Christmas Day, but I absolutely dreaded them. They were a complete nightmare for me because we were in close proximity to my dad and it always felt like he was in a really bad mood because he wasn't at work, so it seemed as if he was always shouting. If I was sat with him and did anything wrong it felt as if I was in so much trouble that my life was over. Like, when I was opening my presents, I was always so careful to behave right, and be grateful, and not rip the paper, because I was scared that if I did anything to upset him he might take them back. So I never looked forward to Christmas or birthday presents because I thought they could get taken away at any time.

I also used to really hate going away on summer holidays. If we went on holiday we weren't allowed to leave the country, so it was always camping or boating holidays in the UK, and it was always raining so we were stuck in a really small space. And it seemed to me that my dad didn't like noises, that he didn't like behaviour, that he was intolerant of other people, of anything that wasn't in his norm, that wasn't acceptable to him. So if we were going on a week's holiday, or ten days' holiday, I always thought that it was only going to be half the time and that we would come home early.

Then there was our appearance. Bodies were meant to be disgusting, we weren't meant to show our bodies in any shape or form, so I didn't feel I could wear skirts that were above the knee or anything low cut. We also had to wear sensible materials, we couldn't have designer labels. So we bought our clothes from Millets, which sold camping equipment – Dad told us that it was hard-wearing, so we all wore camping gear. And I remember for birthdays and Christmases and stuff we got Swiss Army Knives and our school bags had to be camping bags or army bags, because army bags, he said, were very long lasting and practical.

And it felt as if he was always putting me down. My dad was actually a very intelligent man but he made me feel like I was just pathetic and nothing. And that, to me, was worse than getting, you know, a punch or hit, because you knew physical violence was wrong and that makes them in a weaker position. So he called me names and I was the one who he said was ugly and had no brains. He'd try to help me with my homework and stuff but I was always frightened that if I didn't get it – because I was actually dyslexic – then he'd lose his temper. It felt like he had no patience whatsoever – I thought he could just blow up at any time. And I remember he called me stupid and it was a family joke that I was ugly and I accepted it, because as a child you just believe everything your parents say, you don't think they're lying.

The whole thing was very, very anxious-making, so I think as a child I had to learn many, many coping mechanisms. When I thought that he was going to start shouting or calling me names I used to concentrate on part of his ear, or his head, or a hair, and think of rainbows and block my feelings out completely. Then I would escape to my room to my Barbie dolls, which were my little world, and I'd sit and I'd make my Barbies perfect: I'd wash their hair and make sure their hair was perfect and their outfits were perfect. I became obsessed with Barbies. In my mind, Barbie was successful and beautiful, and had it all. So I had this whole collection of Barbies which were my escapism.

★★★

So when I was sent to boarding school at . . . ten or eleven? . . . I started thinking: 'If only I could escape my life.' You know, my name was Sarah Howes, I had dark, frizzy, curly hair, and I was normal looking but in my mind I was really, really ugly. So I started experimenting on changing my looks and I used to spend all my pocket money on hair dyes, or tanning beds, or slimming tablets. And from the age of probably about twelve I realised that I was no longer going to be Sarah Howes, I was going to be somebody else, and it made me happy because it gave me hope: I realised I could change who I was.

And anything that was extreme was part of my big plan to change. At school we used to do famines for Africa. And I did do a few famines for Africa but then I took it to the next level and I was always doing famines for Africa. I starved myself for days on end. Maybe anorexia is different things to different people but to me I didn't eat and, if I did eat, I'd just have a lettuce leaf for breakfast, you know, half a cucumber slice for lunch. And I carried on like that until I was literally just surviving off water and I'd be really happy if I went three, four days without food. I think I can remember feeling that I was really in control, that I had real power, and I was successful at something. It made me feel great. I had a plan and when I was doing my plan – on the strictest diet you can imagine – then I'd also be doing exercise and I'd really push myself. I'd get up at six and go running every day, and then I'd be playing tennis, and I'd skip lessons so I could exercise some more.

I was also bulimic at certain points so I'd binge on certain foods – like sweets and stuff – and then I'd throw up afterwards. Again, I think bulimia is a sense of control that gets out of hand and you think you can cheat. I was really in control and then I'd think: 'Oh no, I really need something', and then I'd eat, I'd pig out. And then I'd feel really guilty and the only way I could get rid of the guilt was to become bulimic, so I became bulimic when I binged. I remember a friend taught me how to do it ages ago at school. She said: 'Oh, it's really easy to stick your fingers down your throat', so I just sort of tried it once, a couple of times, and it worked, and after that I realised that it was easy. And I think I got to that point – there was one phase in my life – where I didn't even need to hardly stick my fingers down my throat, it was literally completely natural after a meal. And I was skinny, but to me I wasn't skinny enough.

Unfortunately, although the boarding school did try their best – they do keep their eye on you and try to make you eat – there were just too many kids with eating disorders there. So although they did threaten to take me to the doctor it never happened, because in boarding school another aspect is that you're lost, you're just a number. Also, when you have an eating disorder you find ways of hiding it and I was very good at hiding it. I'd go and visit a friend at weekends and holidays instead of going home, so I didn't see my family much, and when I did see them I used to wear baggy clothes and stuff like that. I think maybe my mum did suspect once but I was brought up in a family where things were put under a rug, nothing was talked about. So nobody ever really sat down and helped me out or confronted me with it; people suspected it but no one talked about it. So from the age of eleven it was like no one actually cared: my home life was gone and I didn't have anyone at boarding school.

I remember once when I was about twelve at school, I tried to . . . I can't remember what happened but I ended up in hospital. I think it was the bulimia and everything else and they'd threatened to suspend me – to send me back to my dad – so I said I had a headache and I took too many tablets, as I thought that was my way out. I'm not sure what kind of pills they were but they weren't something that would kill me so it was definitely a cry for help. I can't remember too much of it: I remember being sat in the back of a car and the school nurse slapping me around the face to keep me awake, and then when I got to the hospital I remember rushing around, having a tube down my throat, having my stomach pumped, being sick. And it was absolutely awful, I'd never do that again, it put me off for life. Anyway, so my mum had to pick me up from the hospital and I was so embarrassed because I knew she was going to have a go at me and be so ashamed and angry with me. But she just said: 'Don't you dare mention it to your father', and that was it, it was never mentioned. And looking back I think that was probably a big cry for help but she never . . . you know . . . I would have hoped that she would have talked about it and said: 'What's wrong?' But no one ever said that.

So I just started to run riot: I started running away, I never went to lessons, I used to get the timetable and then write my own timetable out where I'd wake up, go jogging, play tennis, have some lunch, play tennis again, maybe go to an art lesson if I wanted to, then have dinner. I was just doing my day like that. The thing was that when I was at home I had very, very strict rules and a very, very strict father, so when I got to boarding school I thought: 'Oh my God, I can do what I want!' I couldn't believe, for instance, that I could wear hair bands that weren't blue. I couldn't believe that their ponytails weren't perfect, that their shoes weren't perfectly shiny, because we were all brought up in what felt to me like such a strict regime. So I thought: 'I don't have to polish my shoes every morning, my hair can be scruffy for days.' I just realised I could do what the hell I wanted, so I pushed it to the extreme and to the extreme.

And I remember the school doing everything to try to keep me in place but I just went completely wild and there was nothing they could say or do, because nothing scared me because I didn't have this scary man anymore. I've learnt since that when someone is brought up and they're really, really scared then that's the level that they have, so that's the only way they can be disciplined in the future as the bar is so high. So when I got told off at boarding school and they had to go within the . . . what was politically correct or whatever . . . it didn't scare me, nothing bothered me. I wasn't interested because it was just normal discipline and that didn't mean anything to me. It was: 'That doesn't hurt, that's nothing.' To me it was nothing because it wasn't like this really scary man who was making me want to end my life.

The only way the school could really threaten me was to say they were going to suspend me, which meant that I'd have to go home to my father. And when I did get suspended and was sent home, it seemed like he didn't even want to look at me; I felt like he hated me. So that was the only punishment that would work – suspending me – and I begged them not to every time. Why did I carry on acting out? That's a good question, I really don't know why, maybe I couldn't think straight or maybe I had some kind of sick relationship with my father where, after a while, I needed to keep the same patterns going. I don't know.

Anyway, eventually it was too late – the school couldn't handle me – and after suspending me six times I was finally expelled when I was fourteen. My dad was disgusted with me, it felt like he just shouted and shouted, calling me all sorts of names, saying that I was useless and a waste of space. I got used to growing up just hearing the same words really. It felt like my mum was having to keep the peace and choose between having me or my dad in the house, so then I started saying I was studying in the library but really I was going to the park, where I ended up just hanging around with the wrong crowd and getting into worse and worse trouble really, taking drugs. Oh God, I tried everything – apart from trips and things like that – but ecstasy and cocaine and all that. But it didn't work out for me at all. Because I was so skinny – anorexic tiny, probably five-and-a-half, six stone – and then I was drinking on top of that and doing drugs, I collapsed loads of times and then I got epilepsy, which was really bad.

Then my parents chucked me out. Because my dad – who was respected in the community and had a seat on the council, they probably thought I would bring real shame on him and the family and whatever. So they basically told me to go away, they got rid of me. So I spent a lot of time in hostels after that. It was really scary because obviously I was privately educated, I was at one of the top boarding schools and I spent my weekends watching polo and stuff, and the next thing I knew I was in a hostel with a load of heroin addicts. And I'd brought it on myself but it was hard to survive . . . I had to use all my senses to survive in that environment and it was horrible. It was the lowest point of my life ever.

I just wanted to escape all of this, because my life at this time was so awful. So I changed my name: I went to the local lawyer's office and I changed my name by deed poll. I just wanted to get away from Sarah Howes, who was me, who had a bad life and was a complete loser. I just wanted to be someone else, I wanted to change my destiny. There wasn't any particular reason I changed my name to Alicia Douvall, I just liked the name Alicia and then I saw a bottle of champagne and I spelt the name wrong. And I don't think my parents cared as I don't think they wanted to know me. So I changed my name, then I got a job in the local hairdressers, and I left the hostel and moved into a flat with a boyfriend. And then I realised at that point that I was going to change my life around completely.

★★★

I'd been thinking about plastic surgery for a while, after I'd found this book where there was this woman who, I think, was sixty years old and she'd had loads of surgery and she looked amazing. There were before and after pictures and they were like chalk and cheese: they were this frumpy woman who turned into this beautiful woman. And I thought: 'This is my answer to everything: the answer to happiness, to a successful life, to get loved.' So I started planning how I was going to get all this plastic surgery. I just wanted to be like Barbie. I suppose, looking back, it was that association in childhood of her being successful and beautiful and happy. I just wanted to be like her. So I lied about my age and I had my first surgery at 17, which was a boob job. I went to a surgeon who told me: 'Yep, that's great, you can have it done', and how wonderful it was all going to be. So I started on that journey.

After my first boob job I got interested in glamour modelling. I was uneducated and unqualified – I had not one GCSE to my name – so it was the perfect kind of career for someone in my position. Also, it went totally against what my parents brought me up to be: conservative, clothes very covered up. You know, we never went on any European holidays so we never saw people sunbathing in their bikinis and things like that, so it was the opposite to how I'd been brought up. I went to a local photographer and he just cut me a break and did me some pictures for free and helped me send them off and then I got a top model agent and work started coming in.

I started doing Page 3 for the newspapers and I became the facts girl for *Playboy TV*. I used to get £1,000, or £2,000, and I got picked up in the car, had my hair and make-up done, and it was a huge thing. And I got down to the last three for the *Big Breakfast*, I was against Kelly Brook and she got it. I was dark haired when I auditioned but then I dyed my hair blonde. But I don't think it was just about my hair colour, I think it was about me not having confidence in myself – I didn't think that they'd ever want someone like me. I never had the upbringing of feeling I was capable of doing something like that. Glamour modelling was much more reachable.

I think to start with I had clear plans for what surgeries and procedures I was going to have: I was going to do everything to my face and then go down my body and do everything else. But being body dysmorphic – although I didn't realise it was called this at the time – I was almost blind so I had to rely on the surgeon telling me what I needed. And I knew that: I knew I was blind, I knew I couldn't see what was in the mirror. And after each operation or procedure I'd feel happy and then . . . sort of . . . I think the anxiety would come back. For instance, after the first boob job I was happy for about a year afterwards, but then I wanted my nose done and then I wanted my boobs done again. You'd have all these grand hopes and then it was never right. One minute you think it might be but then reality sets in and you think: 'No, it's not quite right.' Because plastic surgery has its limitations, it's never going to be perfect. So you have mixed emotions and you either plan to revise it or go on to the next thing.

So I started having lots of plastic surgery. And, you know, because of the bruises and stuff from the surgery, and my insecurity about how I looked anyway, I would have been more than happy to just stay in and plan for my next surgery. More than happy. But I was in demand as a glamour model and I had to have the money for my next surgery, so I had to do the modelling, I had to do the TV and newspaper work. But I used to turn up for photo shoots all the time with black eyes and bruises and everything and in a way it was self-sabotaging my career. It was stressful but in my mind I thought: 'It doesn't matter, I look like shit, but I'll have the next surgery and I'll look a lot better.' It was awful.

I didn't understand, being young, what I was doing with my life. And to me, my childhood was normal, I didn't understand that it had affected me, so obviously I was having plastic surgery and I didn't understand why I was having plastic surgery. And I got quite badly depressed around this time, so I started taking antidepressants, off and on, from the age of about eighteen, nineteen, and I think the tablets worked really well because they level out your serotonin levels. But I was on a high dosage and I remember being in an absolute cloud, so drugged up, I couldn't concentrate for more than twenty minutes. People used to think I was on drugs all the time but I was just on these tablets and, yeah, they numb you don't they, so you're neither here nor there. I couldn't think deeply, I couldn't . . . I didn't have much feeling, I was just a breathing shell.

I think I started to realise that I might have a problem with my body image – and having all the surgeries – in my early twenties, but I just carried on. But by my mid-twenties I knew that I had a serious problem. By then I'd had hundreds of procedures. In all I've had something like seventy operations under general anaesthetic, including sixteen boob jobs, six nose jobs, eleven operations on the skin around my eyes, a facelift, tummy tuck, a rib shortened, my toes shortened, implants in my bottom, implants in my face, my brows shaved. And then there have been all the non-surgical procedures, like Botox, fillers, laser treatments. It's all cost me over a million pounds. To pay for it I went without food or ate beans on toast, I didn't buy nice clothes, I dyed my own hair. Because I always had to make sure I had enough for surgery; I had absolutely nothing so I could have more surgery.

Surgery was what gave me hope, what gave me my happiness, what gave me function. It was my way of life and it was very hard to have another way of life. I liked having the surgery, I liked recovering, I liked the anticipation, I liked the struggle of it, I liked all of it, everything associated with it. If I didn't have surgery what did I have? It was the way I functioned: it was my oxygen. It was like someone who collects toys and stuff, I could bury myself away in my own world. I didn't have to have functional relationships, I didn't have to live my life like everyone else, and I had a reason: because I was always injured. It became my life and the more things that happened that were bad for me – if I was in a relationship and they were nasty to me or abused me – I just thought: 'I don't really care, I just want to have surgery next week.'

So, you know, surgery was my comfort. Just like an anorexic with food, surgery was my comfort, and it used to work. That's the thing: it worked. I think it was a mixture of addiction, obsession. Like an alcoholic or drug addict, I self-medicated with plastic surgery because it was . . . you know, because I'm a thinker. At the end of the day alcohol wouldn't have worked for me because it's ultimately a depressant and it makes you look like shit so it was never logical to drink or to take drugs but this seemed like a logical decision. But it wasn't a nice thing to be known for. Nobody wants to wake up in the morning and become the world's most worked-on woman. And no one wants to be famous for having plastic surgery, that was never what I wanted to be. I aspired to being Barbie and Marilyn Monroe, I never aspired to be a freak.

***

I was probably officially diagnosed as being body dysmorphic in my late twenties after I'd been referred to a psychiatrist. But I just thought they were lying. I thought mental illness didn't exist and it was an exaggeration. I didn't agree with it; I was still having surgery so I didn't want to agree with it. And I was angry because there was no kind of solution. So I said: 'I'm not mentally ill and I don't want to be mentally ill, I don't want to have something wrong with me.' I felt that one day I was going to get it right, that I'd just gone down the wrong road and I'd been unlucky and met the wrong surgeons and everything else. I didn't think that actually it was my problem, it was my fault, and that I was wasting my time and money. That's a tough pill to swallow and it took a while.

To me, being body dysmorphic is like being imprisoned by your own mind because you're locked into the most powerful thing in the world, which is your own self. And you know, there's no answer, there's no escape from it. Being body dysmorphic is like . . . I don't know, I can't think of anything worse. I'm sure people would argue and say there are lots of things worse, but I can't think of anything, because it takes you over. It's very hard to have a normal life in any shape or form: you can't have a proper relationship, you can't believe anyone who says you're beautiful or good-looking, you can't walk down the street or be in crowded places because you think everyone's going to be looking, and pointing, and laughing at you. You're just never happy with yourself.

And you're trapped in this whole world where you're locked into having plastic surgery after plastic surgery and nothing can get you out of it: there's no tablet and no operation. You're blind, completely blind to what you look like, and you're obsessed with something and you totally believe it. I've been completely obsessed over the weirdest things, like a mole, and I've gone to ten, fifteen doctors, and they humour you, but you have to have that mole removed and you have to have it removed that week. There's a real urgency. And it takes a hell of a lot of strength to be able to work it out and overcome it and find different ways of coping and different ways of living your life where you're happy and using that obsession that you focused on – and the organisation skills that you developed to get all the work done – in a more productive way. It takes a lot; it takes a lot to work out why you're in that place in the first place and it takes guts to change it.

For me it took rehab to get to that place. The first time I went to rehab was actually for a programme called *Celebrity Rehab*. My agent rang me up and said: 'Do you want to go to rehab? Thirty days, for free, and you get treatment, and it's in Malibu.' And I said: 'Nobody goes to rehab for body dysmorphia, that's just embarrassing.' And they said: 'Listen, speak to the counsellor and see what you think afterwards.' And because it was in Malibu they said: 'Look, we have people coming here for shoe addiction, shopping addiction, all sorts of things', and they said: 'We've never had body dysmorphia but we've had other things similar to that and we will treat you like any other addict. We'll treat you the same as a heroin addict or an alcoholic. Just the same.' They said to me that body dysmorphia is treated the same because it's the same kind of thinking: you're addicted.

So I went. And it wasn't like normal rehab, where you have to scrub the floor with a toothbrush, and they break you down to build you up again. It was kind of alternative, so they believe in things like acupuncture, and they combine counselling with massage and Buddhist philosophy, healthy eating, just changing your way of life. In a way by breaking you down, but mentally, by making you understand why you did what you did, getting to that point of opening up. And then they build you up to make you realise that you're not the piece of shit that you were brought up to believe you are.

But it was hard and I ended up running away from rehab twice – no, three times – because I couldn't handle it when they went into my past. To me, it was very uncomfortable thinking about my childhood because I'd changed my name, I'd changed my life, and that part of my life was dead. And Sarah Howes was dead. It was very hard and I refused to do that, I didn't want to go back, but they said I needed to go back to go forward. So I kept running away because I just didn't believe in their philosophy, until eventually they said: 'You're never going to get better until you stop running away from things.' So I came back and I finished the reality programme, which took all the strength I've ever had in my life, and then I went straight back afterwards and had loads of therapy, more so than I've ever had.

I did relapse though and I did go back to having surgeries. For some reason I had all these implants put in my face, which I felt really deformed me and were probably the worst surgery I had ever done. I was just so self-destructive and surgery was my alcohol or my heroin, so I went back to rehab for a second and third time. Because for me, it's like giving up smoking: it's not about failing, it's the more times you try, the more chance you've got of giving up for good. And it was quite hard at times because it was all quite regimental and my natural instinct was to rebel against that so I'd do really stupid things. I'd sneak in some paracetamols or turn up late from shopping trips to get on the coach, so I ended up not being allowed to go out because I'd been punished. Also, obviously at rehab they said:

'You can't drink, you can't smoke', and I thought: 'Well, I'm not here for alcohol problems or anything like that so why can't I go out and get drunk?' And that was the hardest thing because I realised that I hadn't completely changed my life.

But I was on this learning curve and I knew I was going to succeed and every time I succeeded a little bit more. And after the third time in rehab I eventually did change my life. I changed my diet: I became a vegan and I eat very healthily now, and I took away stimulants like coffee and alcohol. I don't go out drinking, I haven't touched alcohol for a couple of years now. And I don't excessively exercise but I exercise every day to make sure I keep myself happy. So yeah, I had to change my whole lifestyle to live my life in a different way and go down a different path from where I was. Because I knew if I started drinking, going clubbing, going back into that old life, with my old friends, then I would go back into having my plastic surgeries because that was my life. I had to walk away from my entire life and everything I knew.

I've become a businesswoman now. On my trips to LA, during my stays in rehab, I discovered this thing called argan oil and it completely changed my skin, my hair, my face, my body: it was re-moisturising, it was nourishing, it had nothing nasty in it, it was completely natural. So I visited the women's cooperative in Morocco and they were such lovely women so I made a deal with them, then and there, to become the sole distributer of their argan oil in this country and started this company up. And so I helped the women over there and obviously they helped me because I now have a successful business. It's definitely helped my recovery and I feel I've got a real purpose in life. I'm helping women and different charities and I feel the power of Mother Nature and how you can work with Mother Nature, not against it. When I changed my lifestyle I became sort of eco-friendly and conscious of my environment and everything is positive about my product. My brand is definitely a lifestyle thing: it's about being happy with yourself and making the most of what you've got. And Mother Nature actually is a very powerful tool and if you work with it it's amazing what you can achieve.

It has just left me so annoyed that I spent all my twenties locked in this whole surgery trip. I'm just so angry with my relationship to plastic surgery, it's unbelievable. I feel like as a child I was let down by my father, as a young woman I was let down by my boyfriends, and then I turned to surgery and I was let down by plastic surgeons. I've said that I feel like plastic surgeons are like acid attackers in white coats and I know people have said: 'How can you compare yourself to somebody who's been attacked?' Well, I can actually because I was attacked myself when I was fourteen years old – I was bottled in the face – so I know what it's like to be attacked. And it's worse when it's the doctors who you feel are doing the attacking. I think it's the trust issue because you have to put your trust in the doctors, because if you can't trust a doctor then who can you trust? But there are surgeons who I think are literally just driven by money and who have made me worse off than when I started. I just wish that they had been more responsible towards me; they should have offered me counselling.

So I'd say to anyone who has suffered from the same issues as me – the eating disorders, the body dysmorphia – just get help. If you're in that whole trapped world then demand counselling. You think you can do it yourself but you can't. You know, I started trying to get help by reading self-help books but the problem is the pages are blank because you don't have the skills and the tools to be able to work it out and understand it. You need someone to be able to direct your thoughts in the right direction. In America it's normal – over there they're not shy, they're not embarrassed about asking for help – but we're very stiff upper lip, you know, soldier on. What's our saying: 'Keep calm and carry on?' Don't. You don't need to. Go and ask for help. Go and get some counselling.

I would say I've been cured now for about a year and a half, two years. It's a fragile recovery though, I'm still on the journey of recovery, but I'm on the right path now I feel. I worked through why I had the surgery, why I had been depressed, and it was a tough pill to swallow, but actually I realised that I was good enough in myself and I was an intelligent person and it made me believe in myself. So I didn't need the tablets anymore, I didn't need the surgery anymore, because I believed in myself. And if I fall down and I do have surgery then, as any alcoholic or heroin addict will tell you, it's not the end of the world. I'm still on that journey. But I'm actually more happy with myself now than I've ever been. I'm just concentrating on positives in my life; I live my life in a bubble of positivity.

★★★

One month later we spoke to Alicia again after seeing reports in the newspaper that she had had more plastic surgery . . .

★★★

At the end of the day, putting aside the body dysmorphia and my addiction, the fact is I think I've had some pretty horrendous surgery. The worst surgery for me was the awful implants that I had put in my face, which were actually really painful, and with the chin implants it felt like I could hardly move my face at all. Also, during another of my surgeries, a major nerve was cut on one side of my face so I couldn't move my mouth properly and it looked like I'd had a stroke all the time. And it just got to the point where it was very soul-destroying and hard to carry on living like that. Even though I'd adapted my life not to rely on my looks – now that I've got a skincare company my looks don't matter either way – I still couldn't look in the mirror without getting very upset and having a sinking feeling. I hated, I really hated, looking in the mirror.

Then a friend who I'd met in a plastic surgery waiting office whose whole life, like mine, had been destroyed by having plastic surgery, recommended a new surgeon who'd done corrective work on her which she was really pleased with. So I saw the results and I thought: 'Yep, I'll take a chance and see him.' So I went, even though I didn't really have much intention of having anything done because I felt like I wasn't going to have any more surgery. But after I talked to him and another surgeon who he brought in – who is an expert in maxillofacial surgery – and they told me what they could do, I started to think about it. They said: 'There's an operation which we haven't done before which we could try to do to correct the nerve damage, which is to attempt to suspend the lip, to staple it up.' It was basically a trial, a fifty–fifty chance to see if it would work. And they were very responsible, they gave me counselling and a psychiatric assessment, so they were really careful. They said: 'We wouldn't be suggesting this unless we really thought we could help you.'

But I had to consider it carefully because it was a big operation, an eight-hour operation, and, obviously, it was going forward with more surgery. And that's why I had to make a really careful decision about this reconstructive surgery, because it's like an alcoholic walking into a pub and drinking water. And some would say: 'You know what? Be happy with how you are', but unfortunately I couldn't be. So I thought: 'I've got one more chance, I'm going to take another gamble.' And of course there was that question in my mind, where I kind of thought: 'Am I doing it for the right reasons?' It's a question that I don't think anybody can answer really – what's acceptable and what's not – because it's a fine line, that line of whether it's plastic or recon. And because I'm addicted to plastic surgery that hope did come back and I couldn't help thinking: 'Yeah, this is going to be really great, the result's going to be perfect.' And I had to keep grounding myself and stopping that mindset, realising that it wasn't about looking better, it was about damage control and getting back to where I was in the beginning. It wasn't going to make me look better *per se*, it was going to take me back to when my face moved more naturally.

So I spent my last bit of savings, that were meant to be for my company, to take a gamble and have this last surgery. And basically I had all the implants taken out: my chin implants, nose implants, the implant underneath my nose, my cheek implants. Oh, also, because when they take the implants out it leaves your skin saggy, they had to basically give me a facelift, which meant that they had to break my jaw in two places, bring my jaw forward, and take my ears off. And then I had my lips lifted and the muscles in my face tightened. Overall it has made a huge difference, I'm so much happier without having the implants and my face is moving a lot better.

And probably it is a step closer to me getting addicted to having plastic surgery again, because after the surgery I would wake up and see the results and think: 'That looks good', and those thoughts keep coming back even now: 'Oh, I'll get my boobs done.' But with the support I've got around me now I feel like I'm in a positive place and I'm not going to go down that road. Before, when I looked in the mirror I couldn't recognise myself at all, but now there's a glimmer of Sarah Howes back again, of the girl I was. And now that I recognise myself again I think there is a glimmer of: 'What if?' Because obviously I never gave Sarah Howes a chance, I kind of walked away from her when I was thirteen, fourteen, and turned into Alicia Douvall. And I suppose there is sometimes that sense of: 'What if I'd been brave enough to live my life as who I was supposed to be and what if I hadn't made the decisions that I have made?' I guess, yeah, sometimes I feel like going back to that to see what it could have been like.

ALASTAIR CAMPBELL

Writer, communicator, strategist

'Depression is a bit like feeling dead and alive at the
same time . . . I can look at that wall and see there's a
very nice painting there, I can turn on the telly and I
can see there's a bunch of blokes playing football, but
you're completely disengaged from it because inside
you feel a kind of internal, not death, but deadness.'

Alastair Campbell was born in 1957 in Yorkshire and
was educated at Cambridge University, where he read
modern languages. After graduating he went into journalism,
starting on regional papers, before being hired by the *Mirror*
in 1982 and then moving to *Today*. After suffering a nervous
breakdown brought on by stress and excessive drinking, he
went back to journalism, before becoming Tony Blair's press
secretary in 1994. After the Labour Party won the general
election in 1997 he became the Prime Minister's Chief Press
Secretary and Official Spokesperson and later became Blair's
Director of Communications and Strategy, before resigning
in 2003. Since then he has published *The Blair Years*, extracts
from his diaries from his time at Downing Street, which was
a Number 1 bestseller, and has published four volumes of the
unexpurgated diaries. He has also published three novels, *All in*

the Mind, Maya, and *My Name Is* . . . . Alastair regularly appears on television, does consultancy and motivational speaking, and campaigns widely on mental health. He has three children and lives with his partner Fiona in London, where the interview for this chapter took place.

★★★

So what is it you're doing again? Oh, that's right, a book on mental health. Okay, so let's get right to it. What had been going on in my life in the lead-up to my breakdown in 1986? New job, that was probably the key. Previously I was on the *Mirror* where, politically, I felt very at home. I was sort of a bit of a rising star on the *Mirror*. And then I got approached by Eddy Shah's new outfit *Today*, and I kind of instinctively knew it was the wrong thing to do, but the more other people told me that, the more I was going to push myself towards it. I was flattered into it really. I was news editor of the Sunday operation and I think that made me the youngest news editor on Fleet Street. So it felt kind of like a big step for me. Politically it was stupid, as I'd gone from a sort of Labour place to, you know, Shah, anti-unions. So that probably fractured a few relationships, personal friendships in politics and stuff. My partner Fiona had always thought it was a bit, you know: 'What are you doing this for? You're fine where you are.' That kind of thing. But I went.

Then I suppose the other thing to acknowledge – and I didn't acknowledge this until after I'd had my breakdown – was that I'd probably been drinking to excess for a long time. I mean my first warning from a GP about my drinking was when I was still at school. Yeah. And it's like, looking back, I can see that it was a really steady part of my life for a long time. And I did have quite a capacity for drink, so a lot of people wouldn't know I was drinking as much as I was. At university I drank way too much but I know loads of students do, particularly these days. And as a journalist, there was very much a drinking culture. Totally the norm, you know, to start the day with a hangover and end it pissed. That was the way for a lot of people. But I can see now it was just absorbing too much of my life.

And then in the run-up to the breakdown, the kind of last few weeks, it was just this combination of things. Overwork, a sense that I was driving the whole thing – the newspaper – on my own. And I *was* to some extent, as we were so understaffed that I was doing half a dozen people's jobs, but I was doing them all badly because I was always constantly looking to the next 'legitimate' – in quotes – reason to have a drink. And then the other thing that was happening was that I was starting to get really wired – you know, that sense of a kind of excessive stress, which I've known lots of other times in my life. And I think sometimes you can turn that into a creative force, and I certainly convinced myself that I could at the time. And I *was* quite creative – I was having some good ideas – but some were off the wall. So a combination, I'd say, of work, drink, a new environment where I didn't feel comfortable, all of that leading to pressures with Fiona: you know, a lot of late-night rows on the phone because I wasn't home and I was pissed and all that.

The final kind of spiral down was the weekend before the publication of the first issue of the newspaper. So there was all this planning – quite exciting in its own way – and although I was news editor, I was doing a lot of the stories myself. And I thought it would be quite good, because of the political thing, to get something from Labour in the first one. So I persuaded Neil Kinnock – he didn't want to do it – but I persuaded him to let me spend the weekend of the Scottish Labour Party conference in Perth with him. The plan was that I would meet him at the airport, head up to Scotland, just be part of his entourage, and do a big inside colour piece for the first edition. So quite a good editorial product.

The night before – this would have been early March '86 – I had a real mega, you know, on the piss. I was in this pub called the Lord High Admiral, which was opposite our offices on the Vauxhall Bridge Road, and I'd been in and out of there all day, and I'd had a boozy lunch and, you know: well gone. Phoned Fiona about half nine and said: 'Sorry, I'm still working.' She knew I was in the pub, she could hear the noise. So we ended up having a row and I thought: 'Fuck it, I'm not going home', so booked into a hotel – that big one near Victoria Station on the corner – and I got in there after the pub shut and I hit the mini bar. The next morning woke up, felt absolutely terrible, slept in my clothes, dirty, urgh.

Then I thought: 'Shit, I've got to get to the airport.' So I got a cab, got to the airport, and by the time I was at the airport I was starting to feel really sort of . . . wired doesn't really capture it, really sort of edgy. Conscious of the fact that I'm just a bit grubby and pissed, go and buy a toothbrush and a razor and all that. Went to a clothes shop, bought a new – can't remember if I bought a new suit – bought a new shirt and tie. I became obsessed with blue and red – I'll come onto that – bought this blue shirt, red tie. It was all political. Went to the gents, got changed and washed. And I'm just starting to feel edgy, conscious of people looking at me in a slightly different way. And there comes a point where you're not sure whether that's real or whether that's paranoia. But people really *were* looking at me, because it's quite funny to see somebody just taking their shirt off and throwing it in the bin and putting a new shirt on. You know, it's like, to me it was normal because I had to get rid of this smelly, filthy, beer-stained, booze-stained shirt.

Get on the plane, Neil and his people were just a couple of

rows up, so I had a chat with Neil. When we get to Edinburgh they all get off and they'd given me the itinerary, but because I was going to be doing something else while I was up there, I'd hired a car. So I got in the car and I headed off to a naval dockyard in Fife that they were visiting in Gordon Brown's constituency, to link up with them there. And I can't remember where it was but I was driving along and I get on this roundabout and I just can't leave the roundabout. I'm in the car and I'm just going round and round, and round and round. And I'm thinking: 'What the fuck's going on? Where are you going?' And I'm going between rational and irrational. My rational mind is saying: 'You shouldn't be driving', and my irrational mind is sort of saying, you know: 'There's some deep meaning going on here.' God knows how many times I went round.

Eventually I literally had to force myself off the road and I headed to the dockyard and this is some naval secure base, right, and I'm parking my car in a car park and I'm giving the key to this guy and I'm saying: 'Look I can't cope with this car, you're going to have to take care of it.' And I said: 'Can I make a phone call?' Because I didn't have a mobile then. Go in to make a phone call and I phoned the managing editor of *Today* and I said: 'I've hired a car at Edinburgh airport but I'm leaving it at this naval dockyard and I don't care what happens to it, it's your responsibility.' Put it down.

So off I go and then I get down to near where Gordon and that lot are, but because I've been wasting – losing – time, they've gone. So I thought: 'I can't drive', so I get a cab and I'm now feeling really kind of, you know, like I say wired doesn't get it. Just really, a sense of almost like a hum inside me that was going 'whir, edge, edge, edge'. I get to the edge of Perth, so quite a long cab ride, get to Perth, and . . . where did I go? I went to this hotel where I knew they were staying, and now there's going to be this conference, meeting loads of people I know. I've spoken to lots of them since who say there was something really weird going on, they couldn't work it out. I remember I bumped into this guy I knew who was a journalist, but he was also a priest, and I can remember him being really concerned, you know: 'Are you alright?' and: 'You don't look well.' And I was: 'I'm fine, I'm fine, I'm fine.' And Patricia Hewitt, who was Neil's press secretary then, said twice: 'Are you okay?' But when that happens you sort of take out of it what you want, so I'm thinking she's saying: 'Are you getting enough access? Is this working out for you?' So I'm saying: 'Yeah, I'm fine.'

On the next bit we went to Falkirk and we were in this car and I can vividly remember talking about whether Tony or Gordon would be the next leader of the Labour Party. I vividly remember this discussion. Get to Falkirk, had a drink there in this little Labour club. Back in the cars, got to Hamilton, Neil went off to this dinner he was doing. And I'm just feeling kind of really, totally spaced out, really weird, and asked this guy – it was in the Hamilton council building – asked this guy if I could use the phone. And he took me into this office and I'm trying to phone home, trying to phone Fiona, no reply, trying to phone my parents, no reply, trying to phone all my friends, no reply. What I discovered later was that you had to press 9 for an outside line so I'm just getting an empty switchboard. So that was making me feel more and more panicky.

So I walk down these stairs into this kind of foyer and now anybody who is walking by, I'm reading something into it. People: 'Are you okay?' Me: 'What are you after?' So, very paranoid. Then I'm starting to hear kind of noises in my head, a lot of voices, a lot of music, a lot of stuff going on. And I had this bag with me, a sort of black bag that I took everywhere, and I don't know what I was doing, or why I was doing it, but

I started to empty it. Then I started to empty my pockets. I was thinking of things I didn't need. I didn't need money – what would I need money for? – I threw away my passport. I think what was going on was that I thought I was being tested in some way, that I was being watched. I was being tested by something or somebody and I had to show I could survive. And the act of survival required me to get rid of worldly goods. And I don't know if I was going to go the whole hog and take my clothes off, I don't know what I was going to do, because these two coppers – these two plain clothes coppers – came up and one of them said: 'Are you alright?' And I said: 'No, I don't think I am.' And they said: 'I think you'd better come with us.'

So I get in the car with them and they took me to the police station and put me in a cell. From what I can remember there was this really funny bit where I get in the cell and I take all my clothes off and I was just sort of writing on the walls. Whenever I see graffiti on walls in prison cells in films now I think: 'Yeah.' The two coppers that took me in there were perfectly nice, they spoke to the guy on the desk and said: 'Look, he's not very well, we're worried about him, he says he's this and he says he's that.' I'd said to them, for example, that I was with Neil Kinnock, which I was, but I think they were a bit: 'Mmmm', so there was a bit of that going on. Later, Patricia Hewitt found out that I had gone missing so she phoned the police station and said: 'He is who he says he is', so that was very important.

So then I stopped being treated as a criminal and we were waiting for a doctor. The doctor came, I chatted to him, I was totally paranoid by then. And this thing I say about everything being political, every time he said: 'Are you alright?' I thought I was being asked if I was right wing, so I said: 'No, why are you asking?' And he said: 'Well, you don't look well.' And I'm like: 'I'm alright, I'm not *all right*.' And then I can remember . . . you know those 'sharps only' boxes you see in hospitals? There was one of those in the room where I was being interviewed and I was absolutely obsessed about this: 'Why is that there and what's that?' Words on walls and things, they were speaking to me. So if it said, like: 'Warning', then it was: 'What's that about? What am I being warned?' So that went on for I don't know how long.

The bit that I find really weird in the middle of this: they found a friend of mine who lived not far away, he was up in Scotland, so they told him that if he came and picked me up, as long as he took me to hospital, I could go. So he came down and I can't remember how we got to the hospital, whether he drove me or the police drove me, I can't remember, I think the cops might have done. And the weirdest thing on the way was that the driver got lost leaving Hamilton, and it's now the middle of the night, so he pulls up to ask these people on the pavement and it's the two coppers. And I'm thinking, you know: 'Was that real or was it in my head?' I don't know, but I remember it as real. And when we get on the road I'm seeing all these road signs; road signs were telling me things. If we see a lorry with a phone number on it, it's telling me to work something out from the numbers and all that stuff.

Anyway, I don't know how they fixed it up, but this is really funny – I was the only one on the staff who'd refused private medical insurance and they'd booked me into this private hospital in Paisley. So we get to the hospital and I see all these BUPA signs and I'm saying: 'What the fuck is this? I'm not going to a private hospital.' And they're saying: 'Oh, it's not really a private hospital, they put all these signs up to make you feel better.' So we get into the hospital, find a nurse, and I can't remember much that night, I think they sedated me. It was a nice place but I was not in good shape, I can't even remember how long I was there. I think it was two or three days in when I saw this guy Ernest Bennie, a psychiatrist from Paisley, and he was the one who sort of made me realise that drink was part of the problem. He asked me to go through how much I had been drinking in recent days and as I talked it through I was thinking: 'Bloody hell'. When I'd been drinking it hadn't really crossed my mind. And when people told me I'd been drinking too much I thought: 'Well, what do you know?' Classic stuff.

So I was sedated, I was quite paranoid for quite a while. It was on the Saturday, I was watching *Grandstand* and Desmond Lynam was presenting it and I was convinced that all these football scores he was giving me were coded messages and if I cracked the code they'd let me out. So I'm going: 'East Fife 3 – anagrams?' And I'm crossing things out and joining up the words, and I'm pressing the button and calling the nurse to tell her. And then a friend of mine who knew I was in hospital phoned up and we were yakking away and he said:

'What you doing tonight?'

And I said: 'Dunno, I'm not allowed out. Read, watch telly, sleep, you know.'

And I said: 'What you doing?'

And he said: 'Watching Taggart.'

And I said: 'What's Taggart?'

And he said: 'You know, that thing about the Scottish detective with the granite smile.'

And, of course, I thought he was telling me the code wasn't Des Lynam it was Taggart, and if I could do a smile like Taggart they'd let me out. So I watched Taggart and I'm trying to do his mouth, you know?

And this red/blue thing is interesting, because it's so much about politics. There was this thing on the side of my bed, a colour-coded thing – a panic button – and I can't remember the details but it was sort of graded from left to right, from blue to red, and I thought: 'What's going on here?' And the first day they let me out to go for a walk I went to this park and some of the barriers – you know the stakes in the ground? – some were red and some were blue. And I was with Fiona and I said: 'I can't do it, I can't do it.' I had to get back into the hospital. So that whole political thing was very deep.

As for a diagnosis, they basically said – as far as I can remember – that I'd kind of had a psychotic episode brought on by drink and overwork. That was the kind of basic thing. I can't remember what they advised in terms of sort of follow-through, but when we got to London – Fiona and I flew down – I was still very ill. I was very heavily drugged up but I was still feeling very edgy: planes, airports, I didn't like it. We arrived in London and I just couldn't bear being there, so I phoned a friend of mine who lives in the West Country, down near Bristol, and I went and stayed with him for a few days just to chill out. They interviewed him on the documentary I later did – *Cracking Up* – and he was very funny as he said I was just talking ten to the dozen about myself and it was all a bit weird and difficult, but you know. So I went down there for a few days, then I managed to get back to London, and then eventually I went back to work.

★★★

After my breakdown I wasn't drinking at all, and I was really enjoying that, and I really thought I'd cracked it. But I was incredibly depressed. And Fiona was finding it very difficult because she thought: 'Right, he's had the breakdown, he's heeded the message, he's sorted the drinking out, so why aren't things better?' And I think the truth – though I don't know this – is that I'd always had some sort of depression and drinking made me feel better. Even though it made me feel worse. So the thing is, because I wasn't drinking – I went for thirteen years without a drop – that was enough to keep me going. You see, giving up the drink was so kind of . . . it was such a purpose at the time, taking it day by day. I had this thing about Geoff Boycott, because he was one of my heroes as a kid, so every day I gave myself a run: it's my first hundred, my first thousand, up to two thousand. And it's like that kept me going. Also, because I had another obsession: work – first in journalism and then later in politics – what the drink had covered up before, the work now did. As long as I was motoring, as long as I was feeling I was doing the job properly, I felt I could deal with it.

So I didn't really confront the depression thing for a long time, even though it was always there, and still is. What does it feel like? I think the best description I've ever come up with to describe depression was: 'It's a bit like feeling dead and alive at the same time.' And I think when it's bad that's how it feels. You're conscious of . . . I can look at that wall and see there's a very nice painting there, I can turn on the telly and I can see there's a bunch of blokes playing football, but you're completely disengaged from it because inside you feel a kind of internal, not death, but deadness. And for me – I can only speak for myself – I feel this combination of the mental and the physical. You know, you feel that to do really, really simple things that don't require much energy, just require a phenomenal amount of energy. You tie your shoelaces up and you suddenly feel really tired. So I think that's the closest I can get to the sense of my depression.

My favourite line in my novel *All in the Mind* – which is about a psychiatrist and his patients – was the one: 'It felt like he'd lived through a storm and not a blade of grass had moved.' In other words, there was almost a pointlessness to the depression as well. When I feel really bad it's like that sense of a cloud coming in: not getting out of bed, feeling pointless, no purpose, all of that. When I get that, it's usually a really powerful feeling at the start, like hopelessness. I can't push it off. I've almost given up trying to push it off now, because I've always failed. I've felt it coming in and it comes in and gets you, right?

I think I'm right in saying that I didn't actually take any medication for depression until . . . 2005? Because I was in the public eye after leaving journalism and working at Downing Street, I think there was probably a little part of me that thought: 'If I see a shrink and end up on medication, will that get out? Will it be a problem?' You know? And I've always had an aversion to medication anyway and I think a lot of people do. But it was Philip actually, Philip Gould – my friend who recently died of cancer – who finally said: 'Look, you can't do this on your own.' And he put me in touch with somebody and I still see this guy, not regularly but when I feel a bit . . . you know. So I do this thing now where I give myself four days and if it's not gone I think: 'Right, I'd better go and see this guy and talk it over.' And we have the same conversation again and again and again, and then after a while he'll say: 'Look, I think maybe you'd benefit from a bit of medication', and I go: 'Shit, really?' So I'll go on a course of medication, an antidepressant, and I've had all sorts and some of them have helped me. Now I sometimes say to myself: 'Would I have lifted out of it anyway?' It's possible, who knows?

The longest I've ever been on medication has been about seven months. I'm on them now, in fact. I was just going through a very kind of gloomy, energy-less, anxious period and the thing is, because you've been through it so often, you know when it's reasonable and when it's not. For example – I don't know if you feel this? – but I find when I'm feeling kind of anxious about things, I'm conscious of the fact that I'm worrying about something I don't need to worry about. But it becomes almost all-consuming, you really think it is important, but it's not, and the more you tell yourself it's not, the more you worry about it. So that's the cycle. And I do think, I've often said to Fiona, that it's almost, not literally menstrual, but there's definitely a cycle to my depressions. They come around and there's nothing I can do about it, you know, and it could last for days. It's very rarely more than a few days at an intense level, but then it'll be at a lower level. I'm conscious of it all the time though. Fiona thinks I internalise it way too much and think about it way too much, but I think I have to, I sort of accept it as part of who I am now.

And I'm not good at hiding it, I'm really not, and the impact on my family life is pretty grim at times I think. Very hard for the kids. My daughter is in the: 'Pull yourself together, what have you got to be depressed about?' camp. And even though on one level that's the worst thing you can say, on the other I quite like it, because it kind of means she doesn't get it and I'm quite happy about that. My daughter is very, very up front, she sort of says: 'What are we supposed to do when you're like this?' And I say: 'Well, one, just generally understand, don't play a blame game, it's not your fault, it's not my fault, it's not your mum's fault. Nobody's to blame, it just is, and try not to let it ruin your own enjoyment of life.' But it's difficult, it's very difficult.

I think from my perspective, when I'm feeling very depressed, I want the people around me that I want around me. But although I want them with me, I want them over there. I think a lot of depressives get this, that when you're depressed, the idea of, you know, a party or a dinner or a social engagement, is urrgh, horrible. Some of my worse moments have been in situations where you're expected to be happy. I can remember once going with Fiona and friends to see Eric Clapton at the Albert Hall. And I said to Fiona during the day: 'This is a really bad idea, I just shouldn't go.' And it was like: 'But they'll be disappointed . . . but they got us the tickets . . . but it'll lift you out of yourself.' And I knew that all that was nonsense, I knew the minute I got there I would be unbearable to be with.

Because the other thing that I think I underestimate – Fiona says it, the kids say it, Tony Blair used to say it – is that I do emanate a kind of . . . what I feel. And I can't help that. So I find that the best thing for me to do, when I know that it's bad, is to try and lock out, and that's why I'll go out for four hours on the bike or go to bed. But even when I'm in bed, during the day, I know that the mood that I'm emanating from that room, where I'm on my own, is coming down here. I know that. And when I'm like that, Fiona's strategy is: 'That's him, he's doing it, I've got to carry on doing what I'm doing.' But it's very difficult for families and I don't think there's much support for families in terms of knowledge, which is often about stigma.

However, although I still get very, very down, I've defin-itely found better strategies for dealing with it. There are all different kinds of techniques you can use – writing, recording dreams – there was a point when I was doing all that on a systematic basis and it did help. I think the other thing I would say is that physical exercise has become really important. I took a long time to get into that, but now I find it very important when I'm feeling depressed – even though it's really hard – to get out on the bike, go for a run, go for a swim, do something. I've got these new wheels and yesterday I was going to go on the bike, but then by the end of the day I'm thinking: 'I didn't go out, I didn't do anything', so today I'll try to do more. So that's important, I find it really helps. And now I think I've found that the gaps are getting longer. I think.

★★★

When I'm on the speaking circuit, I do this thing about rules of leadership and strategy and one of them is: 'Get good out of bad.' And I think partly that's what I'm doing with all this. So although my breakdown was the worst day of my life on one level, it was also a defining moment. And defining moments, ultimately, if used well, can be good. I think I used it to sort myself out. This will sound crazy but I don't actually think I could have done all the things I went on to do if it hadn't happened. Because if it hadn't happened I probably would have just carried on as I was: thinking I was invincible, thinking that I could drink what I wanted, thinking that I didn't really have to think of other people and relationships. If actually, that night, I'd not gone on the piss, not had a row, but come home, had a decent sleep, got up feeling just a bit rough, I could have carried on like that for years. Lots of people do. But I think actually, in a way, the sort of bigness of it, the psychotic nature of it, made me realise: 'Fuck, you've got to change your ways.' And I'm by no means a kind of perfect person but I do think about those things a lot more than I used to; I think about my impact on other people much more than I did.

And take my novel, *All in the Mind*. That came out of an impulse, thinking: 'Well, if you've got all this shit going on, try and get something good out of it.' And if you read it, in their own different ways, these different characters represent different bits of my own mental history in there the whole time. And I really enjoyed writing the book and I love it when I'm looking at my twitter feed – I get a real buzz – when people say they've just finished reading it and it's such an insight into depression. Or when I get letters from people who are mentally ill saying, you know: 'I read your book and I felt somebody else understands.' That's getting good out of bad for me, so I think that's why I look back and think that what's happened is one of the best things that's ever happened to me.

It is highly likely that a phrase similar to 'Tony Blair's right-hand man' will appear close to the intro in the second sentence of any obituary of me, because that was defining in terms of my professional life. And I've done lots of other things since working for Tony: I've done my diaries, which will be seen as important historical documents; I've worked for different causes and companies and charities and organisations; I've been on the speaking circuit; done loads of telly, documentaries; now this cameo acting and blah, blah, blah, blah. But of all the things I've done, the thing that has meant the most to me has been the way that I've developed arguments and engaged in this debate about mental health. It's all about this theme of trying to get good out of bad – so the bad was the breakdown, the bad was the impact that it had upon myself and other people – but what good can you get out of it?

When people say: 'I think it's very brave and very courageous that you talk openly about it', I say: 'Well I feel that it benefits me and I'm really glad if other people feel that it benefits them, but I've always felt really good about being open about it.' And actually it's the one part of my life where the media have been really reasonable and fair and I have never experienced stigma, I've never felt it. But when I'm out and about talking about this and doing the whole *Time to Change* thing I will say to people: 'Look, I totally understand why you don't want to be open about it.' Because when you say to me: 'Where's the stigma?', for me the stigma comes in the workplace, it comes on job application forms, when somebody's going through an applicant's CV and they spot a six-month gap and they think: 'Now what's that about?' So then they ask, and the person who's interviewed is thinking: 'Now am I going to be honest, and if I *am* honest am I going to put myself at risk?'

And that is the stigma. It's the fact that that person, if they'd had cancer, wouldn't think twice about it: 'I had cancer, I had to have it out, look at me now, it's amazing.' And it's: 'Great, fantastic.' Now, if they said: 'Actually, I was a drug addict, I don't take drugs now and I haven't taken them for ten years, but I was a drug addict', or, you know: 'Oh, I had a breakdown', there are some employers where there won't be a problem but there are plenty where there will be. And that's why, in the workplace, if somebody wakes up and feels really depressed, they'll phone up and say: 'My daughter's ill' or: 'I've got to take my mum to hospital.'

The thing is, the way the public think about physical and mental health are worlds apart. We've discovered the language for physical ill-health. If somebody says: 'My mother's got cancer', we all know what to say: 'I'm really sorry about that. What's the prognosis? What sort of treatment is she getting?' If you see somebody walking down the street on crutches, you know what's going on and we all know the language:

'What have you done?'

'Oh, I fell down the stairs.'

'Oh, that's a pity.'

But if you see somebody you used to think was fit and well and now they're walking down the street and they look exactly the same, but they say that they've been off work five months with depression, there's a part of you – I find I do it myself sometimes – that thinks: 'You can't be off five months.' And you wouldn't think that if their hair had fallen out. People often just want to put mental health in a corner and not talk about it too much. And it's extraordinary because there's not a single person in the country who doesn't know somebody who's got a mental health problem, not one. Even if they're in the absolute: 'Pull yourself together, it's all in the mind, psychosomatic, blah', they all know somebody.

I do think things are changing, but I just think they're changing very, very slowly. I think a lot of this is about attitude so, for example, yes there's got to be research into mental illness – and that has to happen at an academic level, third sector – but there also has to be cultural change. I mean, if you look at the gay rights agenda, the way that developed, it wasn't just about laws, the cultural shift was actually really important. So I think *Time to Change*, the current campaign to challenge stigma around mental health, is good, I think the charities are pretty good on this stuff, I think that the whole arts world is very important on this, and I think it's great that they had that debate in parliament (although if you think about it, four MPs spoke out, well that's such a minority). I just think, in a sense, we have to normalise it. And the thing is, it *does* come: I've been going on about cancer – well we used to call cancer the 'Big C', we didn't like to say 'cancer'. So I think along the way, I do think this debate is changing.

And I think, looking back, that's partly why the London 2012 Paralympics was so fantastic, because – even though it involved athletes with physical disabilities – it offered us a new way that we could think about people with mental illness too. A lot of people for many years thought: 'That person is disabled, therefore they can't do anything', and then they see night after night after night, day after day after day, what these paralympians can do. So if we could look at it as: 'What can mentally ill people offer, what talents do they have?' As opposed to: 'They're mentally ill, they have none.' So I actually hope that the Paralympics changed attitudes in relation to mental health as well as physical health. Because I think what my whole argument in this area is about is trying to get parity.

So I'd say to employers: 'Respect it for what it is.' I think they should see it no differently to any other disclosure that's on a CV. As part of the *Time to Change* campaign we do this thing called *Dine to Change* in which Sue Baker and I have gone out and done dinners with employers about this issue. We did a really good one in Yorkshire with these real hard-headed northern businessmen, and in the end we were kind of trying to get them to admit that if they saw two broadly identical applicants and one said they'd had a mental health history and the other didn't, that would swing it, and they sort of did. And we said: 'Look, you don't look like a bunch of positive discriminators, but maybe once in a while go the other way and see if you regret it.' And it's amazing how many of them thought: 'Yeah, yeah.' And I think if they don't they'll lose out, as sometimes edgy people can be more creative, they can be harder working. So I would say: don't allow it to define the totality of your assessment.

Take when Tony Blair asked me to work for him. We were in France and I basically sat down and, from a proper kind of news perspective, told him all the things in my life that could become a problem if I was really put under the microscope. And a lot of it he knew – he knew I'd had a breakdown – but he didn't really know how bad it had been, so I told him the whole story. I told him about the voices and the music – and I could see him do one of his: 'Hmmm, okay' – and I told him about the paranoia, all the stuff that went through my head. Basically just saying that I did crack under pressure, that's the truth, and who's to say it wouldn't happen again? And he said this thing – which *Time to Change* used in one of their first posters – he said: 'I'm not bothered if you're not bothered.' And I said: 'What if I'm bothered?' And he said: 'I'm still not bothered.'

There's not one person on the planet who doesn't get physically ill from time to time, even the fittest people in the world might get a cold, might get flu, might have backache, or toothache, or earache, or cancer: they might have any number of diseases of the body. So given that the brain is the most complicated, sophisticated part of the body, why do we labour under this illusion that mental health is different? I suppose what I'm saying is that if you're mentally ill – whether it's a product of your birth, or a product of your background, a product of the way your life develops – you should see it, and treat it, as no different from physical illness. Some days we have good physical health, some days we have bad physical health. Some days we have good mental health, some days we have bad mental health. We're all no different. And if you approach it like that, you do what you do when you're physically ill: you try to find expert help, you get family support, you think about it, you do the things you're meant to do. And I think if we were all open about mental illness then we would all, not instantly, but over time, benefit. And along the way – because of stigma, because of taboo, because of discrimination – that may mean that, for some people, there may be adverse affects to being open. But over time we will all of us get to a much better place.

STEPHANIE COLE

Actor

'I just became so anxious about everything. I was a walking jelly. Some anxiety is copeable with, it's containable – you know, slightly raised heartbeat, breathing, slight nausea, slight over-reaction to loud noises – but in my thirties it wasn't like that, it was that times a million.'

Stephanie Cole was born in Warwickshire in 1941 and started her training as an actor at the Bristol Old Vic Theatre School at the age of sixteen. Since her stage debut at seventeen, she has had a hugely successful and varied career as a stage, television, radio, and film actor. On the stage she has appeared in West End productions of *Noises Off*, *Steel Magnolias*, *Quartet*, and *A Passionate Woman*. As a television actor she is perhaps best known for her roles in *Tenko*, *Open All Hours*, *Soldiering On*, *Waiting for God*, *Doc Martin*, and *Housewife, 49*. She now stars in *Coronation Street*, where she plays Sylvia Goodwin, for which she won Best Comedy Performance in the 2012 Soap Awards. Stephanie has suffered episodes of anxiety, panic attacks, agoraphobia, and depression at various stages throughout her life and is a patron of the mental health charity Rethink. In 2005 she received an OBE for her services to drama, the elderly and mental health charities. Stephanie has a daughter, Emma, and lives in a village outside Bath, where the interview for this chapter took place.

★★★

You must have had such a long trip to come and see me. Have some coffee before we start and these biscuits are rather good. Are you happy talking at the kitchen table? I'll put the answer machine on so we don't get disturbed.

Now, anxiety's an interesting word. It's interesting that we've chosen to use that word – 'anxiety' – because it's quite a small word actually. It implies, if someone's anxious, that it's a little bit of a worry. For me, that's what it implies: one step on from worry. You're worried about something and then you're anxious about something. And to be anxious sometimes is normal, God forbid we should lose our flight or fight instinct because that's what keeps us alive. It's when you're anxious over those things you don't have to be anxious about – that's when it's not normal. Or to be anxious to a degree that the circumstances do not call for. It's when our brain uses it when honestly there is nothing to be worried about, when it cranks up the dial on everything. To be anxious about something is copeable with, but this is much, much more, it's a much bigger thing. It is anxiety writ large.

I didn't, of course, know what its name was when it started, because I was just a child then. I just knew that it was very uncomfortable and frightening. I remember a couple of times, when I was going to school on the bus, actually being over-whelmed by what I now know is panic. I remember fainting at a bus stop; in fact, it was not a faint, it was a panic attack. It then came to a point when my parents were asked to go some-where in the early evening, where children were welcome, so we set out in the car and I was overwhelmed by this terrible, terrible panic that I just couldn't cope. I started to cry and said I couldn't go and I had to go home, so they turned around and we went back home. But of course, at the time – we're talking the late '40s, early '50s – if a child behaved in an odd way it was usually put down to a sort of naughtiness. Then I happened to overhear a neighbour who said to my mother: 'Oh, she's probably got it off the radio or television', so it was put down to my . . . my acting tendencies. That what I was actually doing was trying something out, you know, that it was sort of play acting. Well it wasn't, it wasn't. And then it went away. Why, I don't know. How, I don't know.

It wasn't until years later, when I started to have panic attacks after my daughter Emma was born in my early thirties, that I actually recognised what it was. I was very, very depressed after she was born, and that quickly developed into appalling anxiety and panic attacks, which started very suddenly, when she was three or four months old, I would guess. Looking back, it started as post-natal depression but nobody diagnosed that. You know, I completely adored my daughter, I just fell totally in love with her the minute she was born, but I was feeling just absolutely overwhelmed. I was completely convinced I couldn't cope, that I should never have done this. It was also partly due to the fact that my first husband, though a sweet man, was completely incapable of taking any responsibility. So therefore everything devolved to me; this tiny thing's welfare devolved completely to me. And although I had a lot of friends in London, where we were living, most of them had not yet become mothers so I didn't have that sort of back-up. And my mum, who we normally turn to, was down in the West Country.

Anyway, what happened very, very quickly, I realise now, was that I just became so anxious about everything. I was a

walking jelly. Some anxiety is copeable with, it's containable
– you know, slightly raised heartbeat, breathing, slight nausea, slight over-reaction to loud noises – but in my thirties it
wasn't like that, it was that times a million. I think that panic
attacks vary from person to person a little bit, but basically mine
always started with an increased heartbeat – the heart would
race, I would have palpitations – and I would have an uneven
heartbeat which, of course, is a very odd feeling. Then a breathlessness, which leads to a lot of upper breath sort of panting
as it were. Then eventually, because you haven't got enough
oxygen, because you're breathing wrongly, your fingers start
to tingle. I used to breathe into a paper bag, an old trick that
works because it rebalances your oxygen levels, so it gets rid of
the tingling and the breathlessness. Did I think I was going to
die? When the panic attacks were bad yes, because there was
this danger that you would pass out, which is frightening.

They would come on suddenly. I can remember, my husband and I were planning a holiday and we were on Regent
Street, going to the travel agent to book it. And suddenly I
had this – the palpitations, the breathlessness – and it was so
bad that he got a taxi and we went straight up to our hospital,
which was the Royal Free, and they did all the tests and, of
course, they could find nothing wrong. But because the attacks
were very frightening the natural reaction was: 'I'm not going
to put myself in this situation where it happens again.' And
that's why your horizons get narrower and narrower. If you
say: 'Okay, I can't walk down Regent Street again planning a
holiday, because that might happen again', you don't do that.
But then, let's say, you go to the cinema and it happens again
in the cinema, so then you think: 'Well if I'm going to go to
the cinema and that's going to happen, then I can't do that.'

And that's what happened to me, gradually, gradually. So
consequently your boundaries and possibilities – what you feel

you can cope with – become fewer and fewer. It took about six months for me to get as bad as not being able to go shopping. Shopping was the most terrible ordeal. I would manage to get to the end of the road with my daughter in her buggy and then I would have to turn around and come home. Eventually, anything that's away from the home is a no-no. You know, you can't go out to see friends or anything, the flat was the only safe place for me. What triggered the attacks was absolutely classic: anything that was away from home, because at home I was safe.

Were my family supportive? Not really . . . I think they were bewildered and irritated, actually. They were supportive up to a point, but in the case of my first husband he really didn't know what to do, he had no idea. And of course, you know, even post-natal depression, yes it was known about, but in my case it wasn't recognised, nobody recognised it. At that time, forty years ago, I remember it being seen as a sign of weakness, like: 'You can't cope with your life, what's the problem with you?' There was that sort of feeling abroad, there was still very much a sort of 'pull yourself together' attitude. But you can't just pull yourself together, you actually can't, and it's not your fault. It's just ill luck really. But now, forty years later, we know so much more, we talk about things so much more. Now, for instance, if my daughter started to exhibit any of those symptoms I would, of course, immediately – because the knowledge is out there – say: 'Come on sweetheart, we're going to see the doctor, because I think that's what you've got.' But people didn't know so, yes, bewildered and impatient is what my family were, I think.

And for the person going through it, if you don't know what it is – which I didn't for a long time – it's very frightening. It took quite a long time for somebody to say: 'Actually, what you're having is panic attacks.' Eventually I went to our family doctor and interestingly – remember this was forty years ago but she was a wise old bird – she said: 'What I think this is, is panic attacks, as you've got a lot of pressures on you.' But at first I was very unwilling to believe it, very unwilling. I refused to believe that it was not something physical, because that's how it manifested itself. Because the fear didn't come first, the physical symptoms came first. And I had various tests – testing the heart and so forth – which, of course, were absolutely fine, but I still didn't believe her and, therefore, the reason I didn't get help in the first place was my own fault.

I actually went so far as to change doctors and, after a time, I did actually get the help I needed. At first I was given Valium, which was useless, it just made everything . . . it made it worse actually. It didn't do much for the panic attacks and I just felt that I was swimming six feet under the surface of the sea. It was just a horrid feeling. It did nothing. This went on for some months and then I remember waking up one morning – and this was my saviour – and I was angry, I was so angry. So I got my beloved daughter up, I made breakfast for everybody, and I said to my husband: 'I'm going running.' And I literally didn't think, I just put on some trainers and I went out the front door and I ran twice round the block, very fast. Don't ask me why I did it; even leaving the house at that point was pretty scary, the panic had set in big time. And I just ran round the block twice to absolutely tire myself out.

I suppose I must have just woken that morning and I literally blew my top. I was really, really angry that my life was so cur-tailed, so deeply curtailed; I was so angry that my life had been made so small. I was only about thirty-three. What sort of life was this? I had turned down jobs, I couldn't even shop! I mean it really was terrible and I thought: 'Jesus Christ, this can't be right.' I can remember thinking: 'This is ridiculous, I can't go on like this, I've got my whole life in front of me, what the bloody hell is going on, nobody can help me.' My life had been taken away from me and it's terrible when someone's life is taken away and it actually is a truly physical thing. It's not to be made light of because, when it happens to you, it is as . . . what is the word? What I'm trying to do is liken it to, you know, something physical. I remember after my second husband died I broke my ankle and getting around was very hard. For people who are stuck indoors who cannot, or who dare not, go out, it feels the mental equivalent of getting your legs blown off.

And my anger at this made me turn the corner: when I was so angry that my mind, or whatever this was, had done this to me, that I just ran round the block. And if you harness the energy from that anger it is the most wonderful thing. The danger is that you get angry inwardly which makes it worse, but I didn't, I got angry outwardly at last and to be honest that was what made the difference. When I got back from my run I rang the doctor and I got an appointment that day and I went in and I took the Valium and I . . . actually, no, I'd thrown the Valium down the loo because I was so angry. So I went to the doctor and I said: 'It's useless, I want . . . there must be some help out there.' And he was a great doctor actually, he was a wonderful doctor, because he really listened, he was a brilliant diagnostician, he was one of the best diagnosticians I've ever met. And he said: 'Right, I'm going to send you to the Royal Free because I believe they've got this thing they've not long set up', which I think was to do with fear of flying, but I'm not absolutely certain. Anyway, they gave me this set of exercises that I then took away and did every night, without fail, and it retrained the brain remarkably quickly. It probably took six months of diligently doing that every night. And it worked, it worked.

It's not actually quite the same as cognitive behaviour therapy but it is a branch of it. It was very simple. Last thing at night, in your bed, lying on your back. First thing you did was tense the bottom half of your body: your legs, your bum, your everything. Tense and let go, tense and let go, tense and let go. Three times. Then your arms, shoulders and head. Tense and let go, tense and let go, tense and let go. Then the middle of you, you know, the whole breathing, stomach area. Tense and let go, tense and let go, tense and let go. Then breathe: in and out to a count of five. This means that both physically and actually mentally – because breathing has an effect on your brain – you're quite relaxed.

Then what you do is you choose something that's very simple. In my case I decided to choose going shopping because I couldn't even do that on my own. I couldn't even go and shop with *someone else*. I couldn't shop, period. So I decided I would go shopping on my own to start with, in my head, which was a short journey, an easy journey. I decided to do it without my daughter first, because it was an added worry: if I had an attack when she was with me, what would happen to her? And actors are used to imagining things very quickly, very easily – but most people are anyway whether they know it or not – so I would start with making a shopping list in my head, and then I would get my handbag and put my shopping list in it, and then I would get my wheely trolley. Then I would put my coat on and I would check in my bag that I'd got my keys – everything that you would actually do – and then I would open the front door to the flat, I would go out, close the door, cross the hall to the main front door, open, close, down the steps and cross the tiles to the pavement. Then, all in my head, I would turn right at the pavement, walk along to the end of the road, cross the crossing at the end, walk down the road to Finchley Road, cross the road at the crossing. Then I would go in to either Sainsbury's or Waitrose, I can't remember which it was I used to choose – I think it was Waitrose actually – but it doesn't really matter. Once I was in there, I would check my shopping list and I would go round and shop, and then I would get to the checkout and I would do everything at the checkout, and then I would do the return journey.

Now this took a long time: it wasn't doing it all in a night. I mean, the first night I got as far as finishing the shopping list and the panic started, so I stopped, I did the whole relaxation thing again and I started the journey in my head again. I got a little bit further, but not much further, and I started again. And of course, what often happens, because it's at night, is that you go to sleep because you're reasonably relaxed, and that's okay, it doesn't matter. So the next night you do the same thing: you start it all again. And gradually, gradually, over the weeks, you get to the point where you do the whole thing all the way through. Then, if you feel like it, you actually do it in real life.

Once I'd done the whole thing and been totally relaxed from start to finish then I realised that actually I could do it. But, of course, there was always the possibility that my brain would decide otherwise for me. So therefore, what I did was, I always took a paper bag with me, which I did for some months, and I think the first time I did actually use it. And then I would go back at night and I wouldn't give up. I carried on doing that, and once I could do *that* properly I would think of other things, like going on a journey on a bus or, of course, the tube, or being in a lift. Now that took much longer, obviously, but I was diligent, I did it every night without fail, because I knew that was the only way to do it. And after about six months I was free, I was free of the shackles. I was just so determined, *so* determined, that this was not going to curtail just my life, but my daughter's life, and my life with my husband.

When I'd recovered sufficiently, I was offered a job teaching with a great teacher who had taught me at the Vic School in Bristol and I took it. So, what we set up was: I would drive down with my daughter, she would stay with my mum and dad, I would teach for a couple of days staying with them, and then I would drive back to London. And that worked very well. I'd gone into the theatre very young – I'd spent about fifteen years in the business and I loved my career – but I'd lost some confidence in myself and my abilities as an actor before I became pregnant. I had been looking at my career and feeling that I wasn't getting anywhere. I was working nearly all the time but I could see my peers and my friends, you know, sort of doing television, and so on and so forth, and I'd done a little but not very much. But in fact, actually once I'd worked for six months at the Vic School I went back into it because I regained my confidence with the help of some wonderful people in the theatre who encouraged me.

I still had to be a little bit careful and I still had to do the exercises, but by this time not every night, just if there was something specific that was coming up. For instance, I used them again some years later when I had to fly to Singapore to do a series called *Tenko* and it was wonderful because it freed me of my fear of flying. So although it took quite a bit of time to reprogramme my mind, that's what ultimately helped me – it more than helped me, it actually cured me – because my brain and body were at odds and I needed to put them back into harness again, which I did. There were still sort of lingering gremlins sitting on my shoulder; I could do it but there would still be a slight feeling of uncertainty. It's only in the last fifteen or twenty years, for instance, that I've quite happily gone in lifts and the underground, and so on and so forth. But now it's gone, which is not to say that it won't come back, if circumstances were such, but at least I have the tools at my disposal to actually cope with it.

★★★

I remember when I went back to the wonderful doctor, when the exercises I'd been given were beginning to work, and him saying: 'Look, if at any time you want to go into why this has happened then I can actually send you to someone.' Really for analysis actually, psychoanalysis was what he was suggesting. And at the time I felt that what I had been given was quite sufficient but, because I'm very curious about how human beings work and why they work in the way they do – and everyone is completely different, which is astonishing given how many there are of us – I did, in fact, actually go into analysis very much later in my life, which was hugely helpful to me. This would have been, I think probably . . . terrible isn't it? Lost in the mists of time . . . I think probably in my early fifties, late forties.

I became fascinated by how I had . . . God this is such a long story, I'll make it very, very quick. I had, in my early twenties, met my real father for the first time, we then lost touch, and then in my late forties I decided to try and find him again. I did this for the same reason that I went into analysis: because I wanted to actually have a handle on some of the patterns in my life that I had started to recognise, which were to do with what had happened to me as a child and a young adult. I wanted to have a handle on these things because I didn't want to be at their beck and call any longer, I didn't want to be at their command anymore. Because of course, until the recognition of the fact that they existed, when I didn't realise they existed, they had full command of me. The moment I realised this wasn't quite right was the moment I thought: 'Right', so I went into analysis for – I can't remember – five or six years I think.

I'm hesitant to talk about exactly what the patterns in my life were to do with, because in a way I hate all that stuff that came over from America about everybody letting it all hang out. I mean, in many respects it was terrific, but there is a danger of, you know, disappearing too much up your own arse, with trying to work out what this was. But I will say it was to do with issues of abandonment, of being abandoned twice by my father, of being abandoned at a very young age at school. I had been brought up in a tiny village in north Devon – we were bombed out from Solihull in the war – and I had gone to boarding school from the age of five. And although it was a tiny, lovely school – and we were very, very well looked after and cared for there – it was a very early age to be wrested from your mother, which was horrible. Then my mother remarried and we moved, when I was about eight or nine, to between Bristol and Bath and I went to a boarding school in Bristol – which was ghastly – before becoming a day girl.

So it was all to do with that: abandonment, feeling not able to cope. So what I actually wanted to do was work out what it was and, therefore, how I could actually reprogramme myself so it didn't do me harm any longer. And that was what happened. It was helpful because although I'd dealt with the physical stuff with the exercises, it was only in a superficial way. It's rather like having a very nasty cut on your arm and what they do is they sew it up and they put a bandage on it and that's fine, that's taken care of it. But then actually the process is much slower because then the body has to heal the scar, heal the wound, and then you have some scar tissue left. And sometimes what happens is you have some very obvious scar tissue left and that can be ugly if it's on your face, so you think perhaps you'll have more surgery to take that away, and you have to deal with that. So the wound had been sewn up but there was still some scar tissue and I wanted to just get rid of that. It's not a terribly good analogy but it'll have to do.

I realised through analysis that my coping mechanism as a child and, I have to say, even now – although I know I'm doing it now, so I have a handle on it – is to cut off. Quite simply to cut off, that's it: boom. So I have to be very careful. I remember when my mother died that was awful, but it was sort of in the natural order of things as she was in her mid-eighties. But when my second husband died comparatively young – he was sixty-eight, which is no age now, and we'd only been together about eight years – I had to be very careful not to just pop it in a box. To start with, the grief was so overwhelming that there was no way I could have popped it in a box, no way at all, thank God. But as I went through the stages, in a way I quite deliberately sometimes opened the wound, because I knew there was more muck to be got out. I would do it quietly on my own, I hasten to add.

And at that time, interestingly, what came back was a fear of leaving home. I did do it, and I didn't get panic attacks, but I remember once driving from here, just outside Bath, over to Suffolk, to friends. They had started this charity to do with the green movement and they did, and are still doing, the most wonderful work. And I'd said that I would do a speech for opening this particular thing and I remember getting in the car and I literally cried for four and a half hours to Suffolk. I cried and I screamed because I didn't want to leave home. And I knew this was ridiculous: I knew I had to do it, I knew it would be fine, and I knew I would be home. And indeed the moment I got there – I didn't tell them – and they were lovely and other things happened to take my mind off the whole thing, I was fine. I spent the night there, we had a lovely time, and I got in my car and I drove home and I was fine.

This is going to sound crazy but because I trained in the theatre – I went to the Vic School at sixteen and a half – one of the things you learn is: 'You get there and you perform.' Now, actually I have to say that there's a part of me that thinks: 'Bollocks to that, if I've broken my leg, sod the performance.' You know? But nevertheless, there is something in me that's been trained to think: 'If you say you're going to do something then you do it.' No, don't let's call it professionalism because it's quite simply a programmed response, learned through having been an actor. You know, it doesn't matter what you feel like: you go, you get there. I know the ludicrous side of that, don't think I don't know, that under certain circumstances that is ludicrous. Nevertheless, unless it is *obviously* ludicrous, it is a programmed response that my body follows through. And it doesn't do me any harm – it is a useful response. Because, as a matter of fact, when I got to Suffolk I had a lovely time, I did what I said I was going to do, and I was glad I did it because what they're doing is lovely. And I came home and I felt much stronger for having done it.

★★★

Around that time I also suffered from depression, which hasn't happened to me very often, thank God, and I don't have the very, very bad sort. It's just been a couple of times in my life when I've simply said: 'I can't cope.' I had a very difficult time around about the time of my menopause, when my mother was also very ill, as well as my first husband. And my daughter was coping with that and I should have been doing more to help her, but because my actual physical presence with my first husband made it worse, it was a very, very difficult time. I had it then probably for only about six months, and then I had it again about a year after my second husband Peter died, when I could feel myself actually going down the slippery slope of not coping, again then for only about six months. I'm lucky in that the first set of exercises I was given worked for me, then the talking technique worked for me, and everything I've learned from both of those has been immeasurably useful. So when I started to go into what I recognised as something that was abnormal − you know, it was not normal grief, it was something abnormal − I could do something about it. Although sometimes, of course, it takes someone outside who has to say to you: 'Sorry, stop right here.' And I think the last time it happened it was my daughter who said: 'Mum, I think you just need to go and get help.'

You know, we all have moments in our lives when we're sad, we're happy, we're depressed, we're joyful − all these things, they're transitory, they're part of being alive. So we'll say, in everyday life: 'I'm a bit depressed today', and it will mean you're a little bit low, and everybody goes through that and it's part of being a human being. What we need to know is when we step out of that passing depression into something that is much worse, that is a real black dog. I prefer to call it that: a black dog. And it's terrifying and it's bleak and it's all-embracing, just as panic attacks are bleak and all-embracing. It is something that leaves you feeling that there is no future, that leaves you feeling unable to cope with the present. My experience? Wanting to sleep constantly, not wanting to get up in the morning, there being nothing to get up for. I mean, nothing tastes nice, nothing smells nice, nothing feels nice, nothing sounds nice. When I use the word 'nice', nice is such a silly word, it doesn't mean much does it?

It is actually rather like stepping into a darkened room with nothing . . . there is nothing. I remember once at the BBC, I was doing a play, a radio play, and we had to do one of the scenes in a studio − I can't remember the name of it, it's called the something-room or the something-studio − where there is no reverberation at all. It is the most extraordinary experience because you get no echo and so everything is blanked and buffeted and it is extraordinary. When the engineers are working in that room, if there's a fault or whatever, they are only allowed to stay in for half an hour, because otherwise actually something in your brain would flip. It is complete sensory deprivation. And I think a completely black and bleak depression is actually like sensory deprivation, because you are deprived of those other feelings and you see no way out. There is no light and it is frightening. And nobody can do anything for you, nobody can help, and it's horrible.

But I've never descended into the absolute depths of depression, ever, so I can't honestly say that I know what that's like, although I can imagine. I don't think of what I have as a condition, I think of it as something that's occasionally part of my life. It's not something I would label myself with – I have a difficulty. I think if it's something you definitely have – if you are definitely bipolar – then that is a label, and actually that label helps you manage. But I wouldn't walk round with a label saying I have depressive attacks because really it's neither here nor there to anybody else. There's a difference, I know, because my brother Pete has schizophrenia, so I know the difference between having bouts of unpleasant depression and what is real. It's the difference between – okay, let's go physical for the moment – it's the difference between having a very, very nasty ankle sprain and having to have your leg amputated. As regards depression, I occasionally sprain my ankle but I am not an amputee. Does that make sense?

What's helped me most throughout all these experiences is finding the right thing at the right time. The exercises in my thirties, the later analysis, and the occasional use of an antidepressant to get me through the depression and rebalance the chemicals in my mind sufficiently. Citalopram was the first SSRI I tried and it worked for me and I haven't needed it since, oh, about six years ago. I had no problems coming off it, it was a mild withdrawal, a slow withdrawal, but no, absolutely fine. And I've always been very careful – believe it or not because I'm overweight – about what I eat, because I am aware that what I eat is going to have an effect on my brain as well as the rest of my body. Of course it is, because it's an organ. You know, if I put in too much alcohol the liver will go: 'Burdurgh, burdurgh, burdurgh', and if you don't give the brain the right stuff it will go off on one. I mean I'm not obsessed, God no, I give myself treats. So occasionally I'll have a pudding and I love it – I mean what would life be? – but I don't have a vast pudding every day and I don't feel deprived in any way shape or form, because basically what I like happens to be fruit, vegetables, a bit of chicken, a bit of fish.

And exercise, yes, I've got a swimming pool in the garden so I swim and I love to walk. If I feel myself getting a bit down, then I just whizz off on a brisk walk and it's enough. I don't have to go to the gym for six hours, thank God, because I hate gyms, but I love swimming and I love walking. And so it means, for instance, that if I'm up in Manchester doing *Coronation Street* – which I love – if I wake up and I think: 'Ummm', then I just get up and I pound those pavements. And sometimes I don't and I sit there and I gloom, and I just feel so ill when I gloom, because it makes you feel slightly sick doesn't it? And I think: 'This won't do – get out!' I think I keep being saved by anger actually, interestingly, when I look at it. I mean sometimes if I'm in Manchester and I've got the day off – and I love Manchester, but I've been to all the museums and everything – and I'm sitting and reading and starting to feel blurgh, I'll think:

'Oh for Christ sakes, just get out.'

The dialogue goes on:

'I don't want to get up and go out, I'm perfectly happy here!'

'Okay, but you're feeling rotten, why don't you just get out?'

'Oh, for God's sake shut up!'

'I'm not going to shut up until you get up and get out.'

'Oh, alright, I will, but you'll see, I won't feel any better.'

And, of course, I come back and I feel much better. So that's the dialogue that goes on – usually internally, but sometimes out loud.

***

Have I ever experienced stigma? No, no, because I'm lucky I work in a profession where all sorts of oddities are tolerated. We're a very tolerant profession, because we spend our lives looking into other people's lives and putting ourselves into other people's shoes. So therefore it gives you a tolerance: not only does it breed a tolerance for others, but it breeds a tolerance with yourself actually. And so many people have suffered from some form of depression or anxiety, so they understand. And the sort of depression that I suffered from was within the bounds of normality – which is why I hesitate to call it anything other than just a very bad depression – but I think when we go into bipolar or schizophrenia or stuff like that, then we go into a completely different ballgame, because it can manifest itself as something rather strange. It's like with my brother Pete, if he were to go into another episode I'd know immediately what to look for: it's a slight twitchiness, a slight odd, perhaps, attitude towards something like food. You know, it's something that is very much not within the bounds of normality.

Schizophrenia is particularly stigmatised because, of course, everybody always thinks of those headlines – 'Paranoid Schizophrenic' – they always think it's the mad axeman, and the incidence of that is minute. I mean, you know as well as I do that somebody who suffers from schizophrenia is more likely to harm themselves than anyone else, much more likely, and indeed they very often do. The very word schizophrenia has almost become rather like a Greek myth: it has all these legends and stories around it, which are nowhere near the truth, although they sprang from it originally. For people who don't know, schizophrenia often holds the idea of somebody being in two minds, which is crap. Interestingly, when my brother was finally diagnosed with schizophrenia in his late twenties – although it had manifested itself from about the age of seventeen but nobody knew what it was – it was a huge relief for the family, because we finally knew what the enemy was. But over the years it's been very difficult for him, for the family, very difficult for my mother particularly, who took the brunt of it really, because it was a rarity in that day. Luckily my mother was like me, she didn't give a fiddle or a toss about what other people thought.

But I've seen for myself just recently where I live, a young person who has the illness, who desperately needs help and there is none available, and I've seen how some of the people in this village have reacted. They've reacted in a barbaric way, as if the information that is available – that is in the newspapers and on the television and on the radio – has not touched them. They say absolutely appalling things and they have no conception of what it is like for the family, for the parents, for the person to whom it's happening. And what really worries me is that there is no willingness to listen to what is actually going on. I mean, our local vicar has been wonderful and preached a sermon about how people ought to get their noses out of their arses – he didn't actually say that! – but you know what I mean.

I do despair sometimes. No, I don't despair, because you're doing things like this, and more and more people are speaking out. So I don't despair, no, and it is much better than twenty years ago, it's like racism. But I cannot believe that in this country we still have people – unthinking people, stupid people, bigoted people – who will burst into tears at an unknown soldier's death in Afghanistan, and then actually turn round and talk such venom about this young boy who cannot help his illness. I mean, where are we in the empathy and tolerance and humanity stakes? I mean, where are we? I don't know. It does make me angry, I'm afraid. It does, it does. You just think: 'What do we have to do, actually, for people to understand?'

So what would be the main message I want to get out to other people? Mental illness is not glamorous in any way, shape, or form, it really isn't. For people who are not sufferers, I'd say: 'Just imagine. Just for a second step into someone else's shoes and imagine what it would be like if it were you.' You know, it's so comparatively easy to just take a moment and to think: 'What must this feel like? Oh Jesus, how awful.' Because everybody, everybody, has had black moments in their lives, everybody has grief and unhappiness and sadness. So just imagine that, multiply it by however much you can multiply it by, and imagine it being never-ending, and that's what people go through. But in most cases it's a fairly useless message because a lot of people don't care enough. It's easier to dismiss somebody, it's easier to say: 'Well, he's mad, isn't he?' And then you walk on: 'It's not my problem.'

KEVAN JONES

Member of Parliament, Labour

'The worst thing possible that you can ever say to anybody suffering from depression is: "Pull yourself together." Cos it is the most irritating thing. You know, my line is, if somebody says that to me, I say: "I'm not a pair of curtains." It just doesn't help people.'

Kevan Jones was born in Nottinghamshire in 1964, into a mining family. He went to school in Worksop and later went to Newcastle Polytechnic, where he studied government and public policy. He has a background as a trade union official and served as a councillor on Newcastle City Council for over ten years. In 2001 Kevan was elected Labour Member of Parliament for North Durham. Since then he has served on the Labour Party Parliamentary Committee, as a member of the Defence Select Committee, sat on the Armed Forces Bill Select Committee, served as Parliamentary Under Secretary of State for Defence, Minister for Veterans, and is currently Shadow Minister for the Armed Forces. Kevan has also campaigned on mental health issues as an MP, is a patron of Chester-le-Street Mind, and publicly spoke about suffering from depression for the first time in the House of Commons debate on mental health in June 2012. The interview for this chapter took place at the House of Commons.

***

Depression isn't like turning the light switch off. It's not like one day you're feeling great and one day you're suffering from depression: there are ups and downs. It slowly, slowly, gets into you. D'you know what I mean? That's the nature of it, it claws in slowly, it creeps up on you in small bits and pieces until you start getting to the point where you think: 'Hang on a minute, there is something seriously wrong here.' For me, I think it started to be a real problem back in 1996 but, if I look back, I think I'd actually suffered from similar bouts for quite a while. If I'm really honest with myself, this is perhaps going back to my late teens, early twenties, but in the mid-'90s it all came to a head as I was under quite a lot of pressure.

I was a city councillor and a full-time trade union official, and there were issues at work in terms of the management. I think another thing – because then I'd be . . . what? In my early thirties – I think most people in their early thirties think: 'Where are you going career-wise?' So there was that to it as well. And also, although not a Member of Parliament, I was in the public eye in terms of being a councillor. You know, you think you've got to perform and be on call for everyone, perhaps not taking enough recognition that you should take some time out for yourself. You see, what you do – and I think a lot of people do this who get depression – they actually work very hard and I think that slowly catches up on you as well. I just kept going – you just keep doing it over and over. You think if you keep at it and at it, if you do it enough . . . but you just come to a point where that's it. That's what happened to me and what happens to a lot of people.

I think the first signs for me were, one, feeling that you were tired, because sleep is something you just don't do. I don't sleep long anyway, I never have done, but it was that thing of going to bed at 12 o'clock, then still being awake at 2 o'clock, then going to sleep for an hour, then waking up again. That type of intermittent sleep. And when you've had that broken sleep you can't think, you know? What you also do, when you're alone in those wee small hours, is your mind keeps chewing over things that you've done, so that's the other thing that makes you not sleep. And I mean, I had quite a lot of responsibilities at the time with a lot of meetings to go to, often in the evenings, so you just get to a point where you actually feel very tired. So you're anxious, you're up early, you don't sleep, you're always tired.

And, two, simple tasks that you would not normally think about, or work situations that you do every day of the week, you would start worrying about and thinking they were huge hurdles. I used to run a trade union, do industrial tribunals, and you know, some days you'd get case papers when you walk into the court and you get an hour to read them. And to me I could do them no problem: quick read, just do them. And then I started worrying that I couldn't actually face doing things like that, when normally it would have been completely fine. Then there was also that sense that you're not in control, which I think if you've never had depression, is difficult to describe to people. And the smallest things then get blown out of all proportion – and it's not paranoia, it's thinking that somehow you can't control what events are going on.

Another thing, which is really strange, is that things that you actually take a lot of pleasure out of, you just don't take pleasure out of anymore. When you're in the depths of depression, you actually don't give a complete . . . about anything. Which in one respect, is actually quite a liberating feeling. But it's actually quite worrying as well, cos you've got no interest in things, you just feel that you don't want to do anything. And anyone who knows me, knows that's not me: I'm quite active and I like doing things. So I think that's hard to adjust to, if you've suddenly got no interest in something and you think: 'Why?' So that was an issue as well.

I think when you really *are* depressed, you think there's no light at the end of the tunnel and that is . . . that is a really dark place to be in, when you're like that, and you think: 'Well, I'm never going to get through it.' I think I was never, in actual terms, suicidal, but I think you get to this point where you think: 'Well what's the point of being here?' Or, the point is: 'If it ended tomorrow would it make a difference?' And I do understand why people take it one step further. I don't think I was ever there but I was into that thought: 'Actually, what happens if I don't wake up tomorrow morning, does it really matter?' Well that's the wrong way of thinking about it really. But that, I think, that's one of the lowest points, you know?

★★★

When it comes to getting help I think one of the biggest issues, especially for men, is thinking: 'Hang on, if I had a broken leg or a disease, I could understand it and tackle it', but because it's in the mind you think: 'Well, what's going on here?' As a man, certainly in politics, if you admit to some kind of weakness it's seen as a failure, and I also think that, unlike women, men are conditioned to not show their emotions. You know, I come from a very traditional mining background, which is a very macho type community, then I was a trade union official, and politics is always seen as a rough old game. So it's not a world in which you talk about what could be perceived as a frailty. So did I keep it quiet? Yeah, I did. I didn't tell anybody about it really, because there's a stigma-type thing in the world I was in, that you shouldn't admit to it. And if you actually ask for help it's, like, seen as a sign of weakness. But it's not; it's a hard thing for a lot of people to do and a very courageous thing to do as well.

I went to the GP actually, with pains in my chest. I brought my physical symptoms, when actually a lot of the things were to do with stress: symptoms of a depressive illness. And he was very good so I was lucky, but the problem is that you get some very good GPs and you also get some GPs who don't quite understand. Anyway, it was him who spotted it, who said: 'You're perfectly fit, there's nothing wrong with you in that respect . . . but.' And then we started talking. So I think, again, what a lot of people don't realise if they're suffering from depression or mental illness, is that it manifests itself in a lot of other ways, in terms of thinking that you're having a heart attack and things like that, when actually, you're definitely fit. But when you're depressed you tend to think: 'No, no, people are telling me lies.' So I still thought I was going to have a heart attack even though my GP's saying: 'Your cardiac tests are perfectly fine, you're perfectly fit and well.' But your mind plays tricks with you so you're still convinced that the doctor must've missed something. And that's not uncommon with people who suffer from depression.

Did he prescribe me any medication? Yes. And I've got to say I think it did help me in the early days. I had SSRIs – it was quite a while ago so I can't remember which different ones I had and what doses – but they are quite good. It's not the answer for everybody but I think for me it really helped to get me back down to a kind of level playing field, which is what you need really: it gives you a foundation to work from. Although I would say that the thing *not* to do with them – which I tried to do once and it didn't work – is think you can just stop taking them. You've got to start cutting them down, because they're not like, you know, antibiotics, so it took a few years to taper down the SSRIs. But would I, if I needed them again now, would I shy away from it? No, I wouldn't.

I've spoken to quite a lot of people over the years who suffer from depression who think that if you take medication then that's a sign of failure. I've actually met some people who've said: 'Oh no, you don't want to go anywhere near that.' But I don't think it is a sign of failure – definitely not – so I say to them: 'No, sorry, that's the first step to actually get you to a level from which you can then move on.' Having said that, I also know people who take them for life and actually, so what? Is that such a bad thing? If it makes them function as a normal human being and have a good quality of life, then get on with it, you know? People take blood pressure tablets for life, don't they, and you don't think anything about it. I know that's not seen as the same thing, but it certainly is in my opinion. I can't see why, if someone needs to take a drug for depression or for a mental illness issue, it shouldn't be treated just like blood pressure or diabetes medicine that you have to take.

But although I think these sort of foundations are important – and this might sound cruel but it's not – it's also down to the individual. They've got to actually want to try, and to believe that this is something that you can live with, and recover from, and that you can have a positive life. Which is easy to say when you're here, rather than down, and okay, I know it's hard, but it's about not just accepting that this will be done *for* you. You've got to take some responsibility yourself. For me, aside from the medication, the best thing was the talking therapy, which I got into through the GP quite early on in the process. And that helped, because actually it was just about making you think. Also, I read quite a few books. I know some of these self-help books are pretty naff, but others . . . I read one last year actually which was by a bloke called David Burns in the States. Have you read that one? Very good. It's a bit Americanised but it's actually a good read for anyone who's depressed. So that helped as well because there's some really simple techniques you can do.

What I fundamentally learned is: it's actually about taking stock and changing the way you think, and questioning and training your thought patterns. I realised that how you perceive the world isn't external; how you perceive the world is actually in your own head. So if I walk in a room and you're there and I've not met you, when I was depressed I'd be thinking: 'Oh God, he's judging me' or: 'He's saying things about me', and that gets you into a very negative frame of mind. And that's one of the things that I do all the time – I get quite anxious about meeting people, even people I've known for a long time, strangely enough. You just think they're judging you all the time, which is weird.

Well, two things. One, you can't do that, you can't mind-read: actually I haven't got a bloody clue what you're thinking about me, I've never met you before. So that negative thought is in here, in me, it's not in *your* head. So you've got to take a step back and think: 'Wait a minute.' You know? And secondly: 'Does it really matter?' At the end of the day, what one person's perception is of you will be completely different from someone else's who walks in the room. If people think you're a complete waste of space then they're going to think that. Someone said to me the other day: 'Has your depression changed your perception of you?' and I said: 'No, I think I'm still me, someone once described me as like Marmite: you either love me or hate me.' So how people judge you? Well, I've come to the conclusion: that's down to them.

So the most helpful thing for me was changing the way I think about things, although I'm not suggesting that one approach will cure every depression, I don't think it will. I think there are different methods for different people, so we've got to realise that recovery is very personalised and that treatment is too. I think part of the problem with mental illness is that we're looking for silver bullets all the time, but actually people have perhaps got to experiment a bit. I'm one of those impatient people who expect things to work out straightaway and, unfortunately, I've found that you've got to take a bit of time, cos things aren't always easy in that respect. So don't look for instant solutions because there aren't any. I was off work for . . . what? Four or five months? I think I needed to take time out, to step back, especially as I was in such a busy job. And you know, I think if it takes people longer than it took me then fine. If it takes you six months or a year . . . so what? A year is quite a short period in the average person's life really.

***

I thought long and hard about speaking out in that parliamentary debate about my personal experience. I was planning to speak anyway to raise some issues about how people with mental health problems are treated by the welfare system, but then I thought: 'Well, if I don't say anything about my own situation then actually I will feel a bit of a fraud.' And no one would have known, but I would have known. And people say: 'It's easy for people in the public eye to do it.' Well, I think it's pretty hard actually, to be honest. But I think people talking about it *does* help and, I mean, if we could get to a situation like with the prime minister of Norway who talked publicly about his depression, can you imagine that? But why not, you know?

I said in the debate that I didn't decide until I was sat there and no, I don't think I did. But do I feel better for doing it? Yes, I do actually. I think the real cost is to the individual when they don't tell people because I think it chews people up on the inside, because there's always a fear that somebody might find out about their mental health problems. Charles Walker and I both said the other day that, actually, it's quite a relief to just say: 'Fair enough, that's it.' It actually makes you feel better in one respect. But I do think it's a personal decision, I'm not going to start preaching to people, saying: 'You should do this.' It has got to be down to the individual; if people feel comfortable about it then that's entirely up to them.

All I can say is that after the debate I was very surprised about people's reactions. I can't remember how many emails and letters I got – must be over 500 – but all very positive. The reaction has been overwhelmingly positive. So I do think attitudes are changing in this country for the better. And I think part of the reason for that is that there are a hell of a lot of people out there who either have personal experience themselves, or they've got family members, or people they work with, who have. And that's the issue. And the other thing, which I think Charles said as well, is that we're not – I'm not – looking for sympathy, I don't think anyone is. I'm not suggesting that we all get into group hugs and all this nonsense. But I do think it is more common than the statistics tell you it is, and that realisation that you're not the only one helps. You know, if you walk down the street, there's a lot of people suffering from the same thing but you just don't know it.

It's strange actually, on Saturday I was walking down the street in my constituency and a woman came up to me and she said: 'Can I just thank you.' A woman perhaps in her late fifties, middle-class, and she says: 'Oh, I had depression and I'm a recovering alcoholic; I still take medication but I'm fine.' And the key point is: if you looked at her in passing on the street you'd just think she was a normal housewife. But there she was explaining how she hadn't had a drink in about seven years now and how that was part of her depression, in terms of self-medication. But if I'd normally just walked past her, would you have had a clue? No. And there's other people you're walking past every day who have the same types of things.

Another odd thing for me was that some people I've known for many years have come and said: 'Oh by the way, I've suffered from depression or this, that, and the other.' And some of them have been individuals who you'd think would be the last people who'd suffer from something like that – you know, like a major-general, a PLC chair, a chief executive – but they do. There was a good friend of mine, a member of my constituency, who wrote to me and said she's been on medication the last ten years. But if you met her you'd think she'd be the last person to be suffering from depression, as she is the most lively, bubbly character, a very confident individual, and holds down a key job.

So people who suffer from depression are all around us, and does it always stop you doing your job? No, it doesn't actually. It actually helps, I think, in some respects; in some respects it can be a positive. But that's the thing about stigma: that people often view mental illness and depression as a sign of weakness, they think the two are linked. Well, they're not; it's the opposite actually in some ways. I think if you look back into the history of politics – in this country and other countries – there's a lot of people who have had mental health issues who were very capable of doing their jobs.

For me, one of the positive things it's done is make me more productive, because I've learned through having depression – and I think this is in that Burns book – that motivation is actually about action. People think motivation is a thing in itself. Well it's not, it's actually about the action of doing things. It's no good thinking about a thing, you need to do it. An example? Well, take today. I've got to do a speech this afternoon to open this debate and I had the first draft on my desk last night, when I got in the office after about half past ten, so I took it home, read it, came in this morning and made some changes. Whereas before, I'd have been saying: 'Oh I'll put it off until tomorrow morning.' In the past, I'd say: 'I've got to cancel you this morning to . . .'. But you don't need to, you just get on with it, you know?

Also, I think if you can get your mind to think more logically and put things in perspective – which again, some of these self-help books talk about – it's actually useful in terms of thought processes and decisions. Say if you've got a difficult or stressful decision to make, if you step back a little bit and take in the whole then I think you can actually understand it better if you suffer from depression than if you don't. I mean, in the Ministry of Defence I had to make some very difficult decisions but I never thought they were overwhelming because I could put them into perspective. And the other thing it does . . . I'll give you an example, actually. When I was in the Ministry of Defence I had responsibility for personnel so I dealt with a lot of families who had lost people in Afghanistan and – although I could never put myself in their shoes – I think that I actually empathised with them better and perhaps understood better than I would have done if I hadn't had depression.

Also, because politics is a rough old game where people say and do nasty things to you, if you actually have perspective then they're not that hurtful. So I think a lot of people who've been through it say depression actually makes you a stronger person and I think, strange enough, it has. I think I'm fundamentally the same person I was before but I can just cope with situations a lot better now, because it allows you to put things in perspective and things become relative. So it's not necessarily an inhibitor to having a fulfilled personal life or a productive working life, quite the opposite in some ways.

So I think employment is one field where stigma can really waste opportunity: when it labels people as not being able to work, whereas actually many perfectly well can with the proper help and support. But in a lot of jobs I think there's a reluctance for people to come forward and say how they're feeling, cos they think about how they're going to be judged in terms of promotion and things like that. So I think there's a huge education programme to be done, not just in how employers perceive mental illness, but also to train employers who have employees with mental health problems to understand how they can support them when they need it. And, as I said in the debate, work is actually good for you – for most people – it's just the level and degrees of it.

If people do have problems, employers have got to, I think, give them time, and if they have to make adaptations for work–life balance, then do it. We're a time-based culture: you know, more added hours into the day means more productivity. But I don't think it actually makes people more productive at all, it just puts more pressures on people's lives. I've always worked – and the people that work for me – on the basis that as long as the work gets done, I'm pretty flexible. And I think if you treat people with that type of respect and flexibility – rather than saying: 'It's five past nine, you're five minutes late' – then you get happier and better, as well as more loyal and productive, employees. I think if you look at Scandinavia and other countries, like Germany, they do this, and a minority of employers are starting to do it here already: experimenting with different hours, split shifts. And that's the way forward I think. It's the old BT thing: 'It's not about working harder, it's about working smarter.'

I think another thing we have to look at is the pressures on younger people. I think there's a hell of a lot of stresses on them that weren't there when I was growing up. The Internet age means you're supposed to be on top of information and accessible all the time. It's a faster pace of life and people expect instant answers to things in the 24-hour media age. And is that good in one way? Well, yes it is, but I also think it actually brings pressures on people to have to do things. For younger people it actually changes the way they interact as well: you don't sit and talk to people for hours like we used to do, you do it electronically. And although you've got all these friends on this, that, and the other, you're actually on your own. When I was growing up it was a lot slower in that sense, you know? So I don't think that's good in that respect – the depths of those relationships are a lot shallower than they were before. And I think that is an issue that affects a lot of people and brings added pressures. And I see it getting worse.

★★★

I still get black dog days. I don't think it's something I'm, in quotes, 'cured from'. I don't think you are. But, you know, I have my black dog days, but I think I know how to deal with them now. And I think I actually know when it's coming up on me now, I can actually recognise it, that it's coming. It's that lack of interest in things, or putting things off, fretting over things that you should frankly just get on with and do. If it's something simple like, I don't know, changing a light bulb at home that's been out for ages and you keep saying: 'I'll do it tomorrow', then that's a sign for me. So I know when that's happening now, so what I do is I just get on and do things. I think: 'The light bulb needs changing', so I'll do it. I actually say to myself: 'Why are you putting it off, why are you thinking about this thing?' You know?

But sometimes I'll need a bit of bullying, sometimes that can help. Sometimes you just need that. I don't think you should look at people who've got depression and think you should, like, walk on eggshells around them. When it comes to family, they're important in terms of support, but I don't think they always need to treat people who've got depression with kid gloves. I think in some cases, for a character like me, that's the worst thing you can do. 'Go and put that light bulb up and do that', is actually better for me. Encouraging me to do something practical is good.

While the worst thing possible that you can ever say to anybody suffering from depression is: 'Pull yourself together.' Cos it is the most irritating thing. You know, my line is, if somebody says that to me, I say: 'I'm not a pair of curtains.' It just doesn't help people. I mean, if you could actually explain sometimes why you get depressed it would be a lot easier. I keep saying this to my partner, when she says: 'You seem a bit down' – because she's got like these antennae with me – and I say to her: 'If I could explain it, it would be actually rational.' But, you know, I think it's one of those things where you can just feel it, it just comes up on you, it just gets you sometimes, or just creeps up.

My best technique now is what I call the 'step back' technique. I just step back and look mindfully, and if you do that it doesn't solve it straightaway, but you do actually think: 'Ummm, right', you know? Because I've trained myself now to know when things are coming on. So I just think: well, one, find something to do, even if it's just sitting reading a book. Or, frankly I've never been one to exercise, but I also walk a lot now and that helps a hell of a lot. Now, if I get my black dog days, I can walk for miles and you come back and you feel a lot better. And I usually try – I can't today because I don't have time – to take half an hour at lunch to just walk round the park. That helps in terms of, one, the exercise, but two, I think, in taking yourself out of where you are at the moment.

I mean, we're very fortunate living in beautiful countryside in North Durham and on – was it Sunday? – we walked for about ten miles. And it just seems to relax you. So that's a technique I use.

I'll tell you a very silly thing I also do sometimes – about putting things in perspective – I love sitting in my garden at night looking at the stars in the summer. I look at the massive universe and just think: 'You're actually pretty insignificant in this great scheme of things; you're just one person and you're here for a short period of time, so get things in perspective.' A spiritual element? I don't know about that, but you look at the stars and think that you might as well enjoy it while you can or make as good a contribution to it as you can. And it doesn't matter what that contribution is: it might be being good at sport, or being a politician or even – I say even – doing a job that you like well and bringing a family up. It's a contribution. People might say it's too logical a perspective but when I see some of my constituents, in terms of struggling on low pay and bringing families up, it's bloody tough for them, you know, and I look at my own position and I think: 'Well I'm a lot more fortunate than the position they're in.' And actually, if you're asking me how it's affected my life generally, I'd say positively. One thing I've learnt very much from my depression is that, frankly, if you step back and think about things, some things are meant to happen.

DEAN WINDASS

Former premiership footballer

'When I do me guest speaking now, I come out and say: "Listen, I don't care if you're an 'airy-arsed fuckin' biker or you're at Oxford or whatever – if you don't tell people that you've got a fuckin' problem then how can anybody help you?"'

Dean Windass was born in Hull, Yorkshire, in 1969, where he started his footballing career as a teenage trainee at his home club, Hull City, before being released at the age of eighteen. Brought back and signed by the club at the age of twenty-two, Deano – as he became known – played 176 games for the Tigers and scored 57 goals, before being sold to Aberdeen in 1995. He later played for clubs including Oxford United, Middlesbrough, Sheffield United and Bradford City, before returning to Hull City in 2007, where his goal against Bristol City in the play-offs saw Hull promoted to the Premiership for the first time in the club's 104-year history. He retired in 2009, at the age of forty, having made over 600 football league appearances and scoring some 230 goals in all competitions. Struggling to adjust to life after retirement from professional football, Dean became depressed and started drinking heavily, which eventually led to the breakdown of his marriage to his wife Helen, with whom he has two sons, Josh and Jordan. After two unsuccessful suicide attempts, he got help as an inpatient at the Sporting Chance Clinic and now has a job working for a hardware supplier in Hull, and does some football commentating.

★★★

When I was at the peak of me football career I was a very bubbly character, always the joker in the pack so to speak. Just generally an 'appy goin' kid. I had a good lifestyle, didn't want for nothing really, had a lovely house, nice cars. Yeah, cars were a thing for me, I liked them, and every time a new car came out I'd probably go and buy one. Not so much sports cars, more sort of like general commercial Range Rovers, Audi Q7s and things like that. I had nearly every car in the book really. I had a wife, Helen, and two boys, Josh and Jordan – eighteen and thirteen year old now they are – and everything was going okay. You know, life was good, everything was going well: earning a bit of money, me family life, being with someone that you love, obviously scoring goals. Generally just being 'appy like, you know? So that was me.

But I never took anything for granted cos I used to work for a living before I was a footballer. I was earning £140 a week on a building site and £100 a week in a factory, so to sign for Hull City in the '90s, me home town club, after getting released as an eighteen year old was . . . it was a big jump for me, and obviously I really enjoyed it. I mean me mam and dad weren't skint when they were married, but they weren't wealthy, so I appreciated everything I got when I did get summin. So I tried giving me boys what I never had, you know? I didn't really care about money, all I cared about was seeing if me kids and me life was alright, that we had a nice home, and that when they wanted summin I could get 'em it.

I think the high point of me career was signing for professional football, first and foremost, as a twenty-one, twenty-two year old, in the '90s. To sign professional forms is something that every boy wants to do. And to sign for me home town club was probably . . . probably the best thing that ever happened to me. And scoring that goal in the play-offs to get them up, that was a big part of me life really. It's every young man's dream to score at Wembley and to score a goal like that on that occasion – to take Hull City, me home town, into the Premier League after 104 years – I knew what it meant to everybody.

But I had to retire in 2009. I'd had a good twenty years but I went on loan to Oldham and summin just went there. I moved on again to Doncaster and by that time I stopped enjoying it, I stopped enjoying it. I'd always been at the front of the running – you know, one of the top five – not obviously sprinting-wise cos I never had any pace, but I was quite a strong runner, and even on me days off I got to the gym and ran. First and foremost I loved training, I enjoyed me training, you're with twenty lads 'aving a laff and joke and a bit of a crack and it was a big part of me life. But I was reaching the end of me career. It was obviously getting harder: I started aching after training and after matches and I couldn't recover like I used to do. Maybe I could have carried on for another year or so, but I just called it a day.

When I retired, I thought I had the divine right to just fuckin' walk back into football. And I did get a job with Colin Todd, as assistant manager at Darlington, but I was only in the job for six months before we both got the sack. But I thought that I was invincible: 'Oh, Dean Windass, scored me goal at Wembley, I'll get another job', and it didn't fuckin' work like that. Don't get me wrong, I did all me coaching qualifications when I was a player, took me coaching badges, but obviously it's not as easy as that. It's like being a footballer: once you're in it's up to you then, but it's just very difficult at the moment to get back in, there's a lot of ex-footballers who are trying to get back in the game now.

But I was alright for a while when I retired cos I got a job with Sky Sports on *Soccer Saturday*, freelancing. I was getting up and still going to the gym every day, and then I was working on the Tuesday night or on a Saturday on a game, so you're actually still watching football and you still feel part of it. But I lost that job. I've never been told the reason why, which sort of did disappoint me, as I really enjoyed it. But it come to an end for some unknown reason. I don't really think it was anything to do with drinking or me mental health, I think there's a lot of people on Sky – without mentioning any names – who've been down that road as well, and they've still got their jobs. Paul Merson would be an obvious example – I can mention him cos he's already talked about his problems – but other people that I can't mention with more recent stuff; another guy who's been in rehab same as me, so it was a bit strange.

So all of a sudden you wake up in the morning and there's nowt, there's nowt to get up for. Depression . . . it's one of them situations, not just for footballers but sports people in general – you're doing something you love every day and you've got something to wake up for, and then all of a sudden you don't. You ain't got anything. Forget about the money, you could have all the money in the world, it makes no fuckin' difference. I had no daily routine really then, so I was getting to the stage where I had nowt else to do, so I thought I'd go to the pub for a bit of company. You know what I mean. Then that sort of escalated to going to the pub every day – not going and getting *drunk* every day – but I was going to the pub every day. And I started putting a bit of weight on and I wasn't training, I wasn't looking after meself, and the more I did that the more down I got really. It was just a vicious circle. It's tiring, it's just so tiring; you're waking up every day tired. I didn't have any motivation, I couldn't be arsed to go to the gym like I used to, because obviously I had a fuckin' hangover.

The one problem I 'ad is that when I went and got drunk I 'ad to go an' 'ave another beer the next day cos I 'ad 'eadache. So it was, like, 'air of the dog, you know, which wasn't helping me. So when I went out, I'd go out on two-, or three-, or four-day benders. I wouldn't come home for four days and me wife would be saying: 'Where the fuck are you?' and I'd say: 'Fuck off I'm staying out', and that'd be it, I'd just stay out for four days. I wouldn't give . . . I wouldn't care about anybody but meself when I were just staying out and getting pissed up, then coming home an' not speaking to me wife for two or three days, and then fuckin' arguing again. And then come the weekend I'd say I'd never fuckin' do it again and then I'd carry on doing it, I kept doing it. Every time I got down, I fuckin' went out and fuckin' went on a two- or three-day bender.

So it put a strain on me family life. I'd been married for nineteen, twenty years and we were arguing all the time because I didn't have a job and me wife was concerned that I was drinking too much, so we was rowing and then I was shouting and bawling at the kids. I was losing me temper, getting angry and punching walls 'n' things like that, and me kids could see me doing it as well. If I 'ad an argument with me wife I went out an' got drunk and peed the bed and did all things like that. I was just spiralling out of control really and in the end it broke our marriage up and it sort of went from bad to worse then. I split up with the wife, I left the family home, and I ended up moving in with a girl in Hull. And I just ended up with nothing to do: I didn't see the kids as often as I wanted, I didn't have any focus, you know?

Then me dad died, me dad passed away, which was a kick in the bollocks really. I'd had an argument with me dad before he died, cos obviously he was concerned about me and me wife. She was ringing me dad up and saying: 'He's getting out of control', basically, and then I had a big argument with me dad for the first time in forty-one years. And then six months later he died, so that sort of . . . that sort of . . . I blame meself really, for him dying. See . . . he had a sudden heart attack and I just couldn't get me head round it, you know, I couldn't, I couldn't . . . I just blame meself really. And looking back, although I don't know when I started to first get depressed – it happens, it just happens, you don't know what's happening to you – I think it was every day after me dad died, it was every day that I was just drinking to block things out.

So I can't really put me finger on when and how it came around, it just sort of come on top of me and I couldn't do anything about it. I was just trying to block everything out, so I thought: if I drink, then I'm not thinking about things basically. I think that I was going in the pub and putting a brave face on as though there was nothing happening, as though there was nothing wrong with me. But I was going out drinking and having a laff with the lads and then coming back and crying me eyes out basically. You know, obviously, with me dad dying, I had nobody to talk to. I didn't really speak to anybody, just bottled things up and put a brave face on, because you're Dean Windass and everybody thinks you're a bubbly character. And it sort of escalated from that really, and I was in a hole and I couldn't really get out of it, and I was just digging meself in deeper.

Looking back I do think that I had other periods of me life when I suffered from depression, but I think it all comes down to drinking. I'm not saying I was an alcoholic but . . . it was a big part of it, it was a big part of it. What I done was if things weren't going right in me life, I'd just go and run and have a drink. When I played for Aberdeen the fitness coach sensed that I was down and I wasn't playing well – I was out the team – and I said: 'Look, I'm sort of drinking a little bit too much and I need some 'elp.' And he put me onto this therapist, a bloke, who I went to speak to and got a few things off me chest. Me parents split up when I was thirteen and that obviously affected me life. I just couldn't handle me mam and dad splitting up, I never forgive them two splitting up. I never spoke to me mam for three years, even though me dad had an affair and went off with another woman. But me and me dad never fell out, I sort of blamed me mam I think, I don't know why. Obviously I get on well with me mam now, so I was just blaming everybody else. So speaking to 'im about it sort of helped me a little bit, you know?

So this bloke, this therapist, said: 'Look you can still go for a drink but just don't go mad, just calm the drinking down and you won't get depressed.' And I did that and I managed it, I think for about six or seven months, and I was fine. And I thought I was . . . I thought I was cured. So I felt a little bit better after that. But obviously every time that summin went wrong I just fuckin' turned round to the drink, just thought: 'Fuck it, I'm going out and I'm gonna go and get drunk', and that's what I used to do. So I was drinking for a number of years really, but obviously while I was still training every day, I wasn't that bad in me early days.

But the last year it sort of caught up with me a little bit, you know? Obviously because I didn't share with anybody, I never spoke to anybody, it was just getting worse and worse really, and the more fed up I got, the more I went out for a drink just to pick meself up. Just to say: 'Well he's the laffer and joker of the pack, look at him in the pub 'avin' a laff, there's nowt wrong with him.' I didn't want anybody to know that I was properly down but obviously when you close that door, and you're in your family life, nobody knows what's happening. I could be laffin and joking one minute and shut the fuckin' front door and next thing crying me fuckin' eyes out – it was getting to the stage where I was like that.

You know, Gary Speed was out the blue. I fuckin' played against him, I spoke to Gary a few times, and you would never have thought that he had a problem. Listen, people think everything's alright, he was manager of Wales, nobody would have ever dreamed of what he did. And obviously, for his family, it's distraught for 'em. Nobody knows the story, and I don't want to know what or why he did it, it's none of my business. Obviously the boy was suffering in some sort of way and consequently it ended his life. That is a prime example of people thinking that everything is rosy in the garden cos you're Gary Speed, or Dean Windass, or Stan Collymore, or whoever, you know, Ricky Hatton. There's loads of us. It's tough, it's tough, it *is* tough. So what you try doing, you try to block it out I think.

***

I don't know how I would describe depression to someone who's never been through it. It's just . . . I don't know, I tended to over-think too much, and everything that had gone wrong in me life, I sort of couldn't handle it, I couldn't handle things. It was like being caught in a dark cloud, or walking down a dark corridor or tunnel, and there was just no light at the end of it for me, I just didn't want to be around anymore. And I thought to meself: 'If I'm 'urtin' that many people, if I'm not 'ere then I can't 'urt anybody', basically. That was my attitude. I just didn't wanna be 'ere, I didn't wanna be alive, I didn't wanna wake up in the fuckin' morning. I dreaded going a bed cos I didn't wanna wake up the next day . . . drinking lager on a night just to sort of make me go to sleep. But then I'd feel rough in the morning and I'd fuckin' go out for a drink again when me girlfriend went to work. I'd just go to the pub, you know, and then obviously drink driving and all that shit. It was just a fuckin' mess.

And it led to thoughts of suicide. It was sort of strange really cos I was a bit drunk and it was a bit surreal and I don't know if I . . . I don't know if I attempted to do it properly or not. I don't know if it scared me or what, but it got to a stage where

I just . . . I didn't want to be here, but I don't think I 'ad the bollocks to fuckin' do it, basically. Nothing was going through me head really, I just didn't want to be alive, just felt: 'Well, if I take these tablets then I won't be fuckin' here anymore.' And, you know, drinking Amaretto and taking tablets, I just thought well if . . . if I just take tablets then everything will go away and I won't wake up and then obviously I can't hurt anybody else. Cos that's all I kept doing, I kept hurting the ones that were closest to me, in Helen and Josh and Jordan. It was a selfish thing to do, yeah I know that, I know that now, but at the time you think if you want to stop hurting people then if I kill meself, or if I'm not here, then I don't hurt anybody.

The first time I was found by me girlfriend in the kitchen, on the floor. Obviously I was very down but I can't really remember it. I just spewed up, then I went to bed, and then I was alright again the next day to be fair. The second time, I was on the landing and I just thought I'll try and see . . . see, basically, if I can hang meself. I'd rang up me friend close to me and just said: 'I'm really down and I'm gonna fuckin' do something stupid.' I got a sheet but cos I was, like, hungover and drunk, I got a sheet which was too long so it didn't work. Then I got a belt and I tried . . . I put a belt round me neck. And as I went to try doing it, when I was just pulling it onto the landing, she walked through the door, you know? So if she hadn't of walked in, then I don't know what would have happened. And that's when she rang me mam up and me brother-in-law, and they came round and said: 'Look you need to fuckin' . . . you need to get some help.'

So what I done was I got all me gear, left me girl, left the house, and went back to Leeds and went back to me wife. Obviously we weren't having a sexual relationship, she just let me sleep in the eldest lad's bed and helped me. And then Ian Ashbee put me on to Clarke Carlisle, as obviously Clarke Carlisle has suffered the same, and he said: 'Look I'll put you on to a gentleman at the Sporting Chance Clinic.' So I spoke to him and he asked me to go down for an assessment, but I just couldn't speak really, I was in tears, and he just said: 'Look, you need to come in.' So, like, I had to go in, sort of two weeks later, for twenty-six days.

When I was there part of the programme is you go to the gym in the morning every day at 9 o'clock. Then you come back and you do a group session and speak about what's happening to people, and I was just breaking down. And in the afternoon you'd have one-to-one meetings, and then you do your steps, you go to AA meetings, and share in the AA meetings, even though I was saying I wasn't an alcoholic. Before, I thought AA meetings were for these down and out fuckin' people, but there's some very sophisticated people that go to them meetings you know? There was this big famous rock star in one of our meetings, so if a big personality and big star can stand there in front of twenty-odd people, then I can. And I actually really enjoyed going to the meetings, cos everybody was talking about their problems and sharing really, and that's what they got into your 'ead: that you have to share with people, cos if you don't you end up fuckin' dead.

I didn't take any medication for depression, I didn't take anything at all, cos I think my biggest problem was having the bollocks to come out and say that I am fuckin' down. It's tough, but when I went to rehab I learnt to talk about things. I never used to talk about things, like when me dad died and I bottled everything up, and that's when I used to go drinking and I was crying all the time, I was fed up all the time. You know, I was like a yoyo, I was up one day and down the next, there was no in between with me. But even though this stuff was difficult at first, once I started to pour everything out, it made me feel better. It was like a weight lifting . . . a weight lifting off me shoulders.

And the response I got when I was in rehab was incredible, on Twitter and letters that got sent to Sporting Chance, from Hull City supporters and football supporters in general. I had a great response from people saying: 'Hope you get better soon', an' this, that 'n' the other. I have had some negative reactions though. A girl had a go at me in me local pub once, cos her dad committed suicide, and she sort of said, you know: 'You're a fuckin' selfish man.' And I thought: 'Why's she being funny with me?', cos I obviously didn't know that her dad committed suicide. So it sort of . . . I think it upset her, thinking: 'Well you've got a good life in front of you . . .'. But she was suffering because her dad killed hi'self and she had all the heartache with it. Listen, everybody's got their own opinions, you know, and she was right, the lady was right, it was a selfish way. I wanted to die. I didn't want to be here anymore cos I didn't want to hurt anybody else.

You know, I may be a big 'ard fuckin' man on the football pitch, but I'm soft as shit when I come off it – that was my personality. I'd fight anybody, it weren't a problem to me, but obviously I looked at meself as a failure really cos, well, I'd lost me wife and me kids and everything that I'd worked hard for, so that's the road I went down. But if I'd of gone ahead and done it then I'd a ruined me kids for the rest of their life. And I think that if I didn't get to rehab I don't know what would've happened to me. Looking back now it was probably one of the best twenty-six days I've had for a number of years, I really enjoyed it. I mean, I wanted to come home, of course I did – I wanted to give it up halfway cos I didn't think I'd be able to do it, 'n' the three lads who I was in with was exactly the same – but I did it and I felt good. Obviously I lost a lot of weight by training and I didn't have a drink for forty-odd days, and that's how I sort of got me help really.

★★★

And I'm 'appy now. Even though I ain't got the money, I'm 'appy. I work in Hull for Quality Fixings, selling nuts and bolts, and I get up in the morning . . . I actually wake up in the morning and want to go to work. The bloke who give me a job said: 'You're the face of Hull, you, you might get me a bit of business and some hard work at the same time.' Even when I got done drink-driving and crashed me car and was banned for two years, he still kept me in a job. I get drove around now by one of the lads in the office, and we go out and meet people and get through the doors and try and sell as many things as we can really. So I work hard, you know, I work hard for what I get now. It seems a bit of a stupid cliché really but the more you have, the more people want to take off you. So, you know, when you ain't got nowt they can't take it off you. And now I don't have hardly 'owt, just a bit to get me by.

Filling time and keeping busy is the main thing I try telling people: that you've got to keep busy, you've got to get up for something in the morning. I don't care what it is but you've got to get up, cos if you don't, you end up going to the pub cos you're bored and eventually your fuckin' money runs out, and you fuckin' end up going crackers, you know? Now I play football on a Saturday in Hull, so that takes me mind off it for an hour an' half or so, and I enjoy me weekends. And I do a lot of commentating as well now with me Sky Sports work on the radio on Thursdays, so I've got summin. And obviously I got community service for me drink-driving. So I work three days a week, do me community service Mondays and Fridays – even though I don't want to do me community service in a charity shop in Bingley, I've gotta do it, cos if not, I'll go to prison! – so at least I'm, like, busy.

And yeah, depression never leaves you; it's treatable innit, but it's never curable I don't think. I have good days and I have bad days, I'm still having good days and bad days. I'm still having fuckin' fights and arguments with me ex-wife about me children, and me children don't speak to me cos I'm back with this girl again now, and it's very difficult at the moment. You know, I miss me kids dearly and hopefully they'll forgive me and eventually come round and want to see me again, but at the moment it's a bit raw, so there's nothing I can do about that, I've got to get on with it. But I'm probably a bit mentally stronger than I was before. Before I was fuckin' . . . before I would crumble and go out on the piss and get drunk and feel sorry for meself. But I don't do it now. And obviously now I can talk about me dad and not cry. Don't get me wrong, I miss me dad fuckin' deeply but, you know, I can cope with it now, I can live with it. But before I couldn't cope with it, I couldn't, you know . . . when he died it screwed me up inside.

If I had one message for people it would be: just be strong, just come out and please admit that you've got a problem, cos if you don't, it could sadly end in a bad way. I'm glad I can talk about it now, I'm glad I'm here to tell the tale – if it helps anybody in any way, shape or form, if I can help one person, then brilliant. I'm not doing this for sympathy or for people to feel sorry for me, it was just the path that I'd gone down. And even though I still have bad days – I've had a bit of a bad day today really, I've been down today – I've got to be positive, I've got to keep fuckin' active and keep working. So first and foremost: just come out and talk and go and see your GP, go and see anybody, go and see your next-door neighbour if you have to. You know, when I do me guest speaking now, I come out and say: 'Listen, I don't care if you're an 'airy-arsed fuckin' biker or you're at Oxford or whatever – if you don't tell people that you've got a fuckin' problem then how can anybody help you?'

TRISHA GODDARD

Broadcaster and chat-show host

'There's no glamour in being a mental health patron – with mental health they think it's catching and they still connect mad and bad. Where are the big balls to do with mental health? Who are the glitzy stars who hold star-spangled do's for mental health? You know, there's no glitz, there's no glamour, no pink or red ribbons, no Liz Hurleys and Elton Johns. When I had breast cancer everyone was my best friend, wanting to come and hug me and saying: "Can you do this, and can you do that, and can you be guest of honour at this, that, and the other?" Oh, I could live high on being a spokesperson for a breast cancer charity, which I will not be. There's far more glamour in that than in mental health.'

Born in London in 1957, Trisha spent her childhood in Tanzania, Norfolk, and Surrey. After emigrating to Australia in 1985 she became a reporter and television presenter, most notably on *Play School*; presenting ABC's *7.30 Report*; and the prime-time show *Everybody*. She then started her own production company, where she produced and presented over 400 programmes of the chat show *Live It Up*. In 1998, Trisha moved to the UK to present the ITV daily chat show *Trisha* and later *Trisha Goddard* for Five. In 2012, she began to host the US *Trisha Goddard* talk show on NBC and now splits her time between America and Norfolk, where she lives with her third husband Peter Gianfrancesco – CEO of Norwich Mind and a psychotherapist – her two daughters Billie and Madi, and their dog Alf. Trisha has experienced episodes of depression, anxiety, eating disorders, and obsessive compulsive disorder (OCD) since she was a teenager, which led to a nervous breakdown and a stay in a psychiatric hospital in 1994. In Australia she worked as a mental health activist, while in the UK she became a licensed Neuro-Linguistic Programming (NLP) Practitioner, Mind Mental Health First Aider, and Patron of Norwich Home-Start and Norwich Mind. The interview upon which this chapter is based took place in London, just before Trisha began filming for her new US talk show.

***

You know what? Madness is normal. How can it not be, with so many people? All of us know at least one person with some sort of mental illness, it's not that unusual these days. In fact, it's everywhere, it is everywhere. One in four, we say. Or, you know, some people say one in one, because we're talking about mental illness, but mental health is part of that continuum. And we've all got mental health and how it is at the time depends on a lot of different things. It's a normal part of the human condition for something in the body to go wrong: it might be a foot, it might be a knee, it might be an elbow, it might be the mind.

With the benefit of hindsight I really started suffering – and I use my words very carefully – from mental health problems when I was around fourteen. But to me, it was just how I was, I was a very sensitive child. The person I thought was my father, who I learnt a few years ago was actually my stepfather, worked as a psychiatric nurse – in the days when it was more about restraint and learning judo – and could be very unpredictable and aggressive. So I always felt I had no control, because there seemed to be no rhyme or reason to his behaviour. I couldn't say to myself: 'If I do X I'll get into trouble and get a hiding, if I do Y . . .'. I didn't know when and where it was coming because, in retrospect, whether he laughed or lashed out was tied into his moods, not what I did.

When my stepfather became very aggressive and got me in a corner and started on me, at first I tried crying, putting my arms up, but that made it worse, it was: 'Shut up, I'll give you something to cry for.' So I developed this thing where I would just go limp, because if I didn't put any resistance up it still went on but not as long. So I used to just go completely limp; we all did, we all had this thing. One of my sisters said to me that if you wear lots of clothes it doesn't hurt as much and she used to wear coats all the time, day and night. As an adult, weight became her issue. My thing was I'd just flop and I'd go somewhere else in my head. But one time he did it, the last time he did it, mum screamed at him: 'Stop it, you'll kill the child, you'll kill the child!' And that really frightened me because I had no awareness; you don't, you don't know what it is, you know? It wasn't on television like now. So whether that was a trigger for my problems – I never blame – I don't know.

I loved school. I went to a very posh, very strict, girls' school and I realise now that I loved it because it was strict but it was strict without violence – there were a lot of Quaker teachers there so there was a lot of understanding. I was really good at school: I was the class clown and chatterbox because it was one of the few places where I could be who I wanted to be, so I could be bright and get As and the teacher would say: 'Well done.' I wouldn't be told to shut up, or risk a backhander, or be told I was bragging, so school was my safe haven. But I felt a lot of anxiety at the time, especially when I woke up in the morning – that was the time when the anxiety was at its worst – so I needed a slug of drink to get me there. I used to climb up to the top shelf where they used to keep sherry for special occasions and have a swig of that for breakfast because it used to make the grown-ups at Christmas quite . . . you know. So I think that's where it all really started, and that became who I was.

I think it's important to realise – I know from experience – that depression isn't something in a box that comes on its own: it's like a fungus that has fingers in lots of different things and I became dysfunctional at eating. And then, of course, yeah, I started losing weight, and then you get compliments, so there's nothing to say that you're doing the wrong thing. I was a bit chubby, I suppose, but that wasn't what it was about, it was a way of control, absolute control. I really get pissed off when people go on about magazines – like coroners saying that this girl died and it was directly down to magazines. It's bullshit, you know? It trivialises it, it trivialises the pain someone feels, to think that someone who is perfectly normal is going to pick up a fashion magazine and think: 'Oh, that's a good idea, I'm not going to eat for the next five years.' That's not what it was about, that's absolutely not what it was about.

Another thing that I did, I really believed in 'four' and four is still my problem number. I got it into my head – I don't know where it came from – that I had to do everything four times, like touch the tap four times. And I never trod on the fourth stair of the house we lived in. And actually when *The One Show* took me back – they did a series about growing up in houses and I took my elder daughter back – I still knew, without looking at the step, where the fourth step was. So I had to skip over it, couldn't touch it. Everything was in fours, I had this obsession, and all of that – that whole thing – was my depression, trying to control everything in a world where there is no control.

Round about puberty I got into writing poetry and I still to this day, forty years later, cannot read what I wrote at fourteen because it was so dark. I was actually, I think, a very descriptive poet – I managed to describe my moods without realising I was having them. When I was about fifteen I sent some of these poems I'd written about death into *Poet's Corner* on the BBC and they devoted the whole of the programme to them – I'll never forget he called me Pat-REE-cha – and as a result I got all of these letters from people. In those days to write into the BBC was quite different and they had two bags, two big plastic bags of letters, that were eventually delivered to the house. And 99 per cent of them said: 'I've just come back from a funeral', or 'I've just buried a loved one', and 'I've just' – you know – 'seen my brother die' . . . 'and you described it perfectly'. Yet I had never seen death, I had no idea. And to me now, looking back, to think that I captured perfectly the mood of people who were burying, had buried, or were mourning, people who had died, as a fourteen year old, you think: 'Where'd you get that from?' And I think I now realise that, at fourteen, you don't have all the social filters, you just write what you feel, and what I was feeling was what other people felt at really acute dreadful mourning times.

And that was me. That was who I was, you know? It didn't have a label: it wasn't depression, it wasn't an eating disorder, it wasn't OCD. It was me. And I think – I now know – having done work with early intervention mental health, that you have to be very careful with words. We all think we're normal and when someone says: 'You've got a mental illness', it's labelling how someone may be coping, albeit clinging on by the end of their claws. But that was how I coped, and that was who I was, and I had a cycle of similar behaviour right up until I had my breakdowns as an adult.

★★★

In 1985 I moved to Australia because I married – God knows why, probably as an escape – a very controlling man, an Australian politician who I met when I was an air stewardess. Robert used to do things like 'accidentally' lock me in the house and he tried to control everything, from what I wore to what I ate. He wouldn't allow me to eat vegetarian food – I'd been vegetarian since 1980, again, that became my control food – so every meal time was a battlefield. And then I found out that he was playing all sorts of mind games, like going through my address book and ringing up my friends and saying 'I'm worried about her' – I was probably going through a depressive stage – and getting them to spy on me. He was finding out what I'd said to them and then he'd drop it into conversations. And that's when I really thought: 'I'm going mad.' Because how is it he knows my thoughts? Eventually one of my best friends, Noel, who I went to the gym with, opened up to me and said Robert had sat down with him and had drawn up some plan that he would basically pay Noel to sleep with me so he didn't lose me, as by this time we had no sex life and slept in separate beds, and . . . oh, all this.

And I used to be one of those people – and I still am, but not as bad – who never lost their temper, which means that anger becomes internalised. I had a lot of rage from the bursts of anger I'd seen as a child against me. So, anyway, I completely lost it, and I walked – ran – home from Noel's flat with Noel running after me, saying: 'Don't tell him I told you.' I was ranting and raving and screaming, I'd had a couple of glasses of wine, and that was it. I got in and Robert started on me again and there was a flashpoint when I had picked up this knife and he started with: 'Oh no, you're quite mad', and I always say that if I hadn't slashed my wrists I know I would have killed him. I know I would have stabbed him. It's not dramatics: I was at such a pitch, I was alienated from everyone I knew, I didn't know who I could trust because of his behaviour, and he was a politician so he was very slick and what have you. Suddenly I was being called mad, I was frightened, I was angry, and – *bang!* – you know? I absolutely see how someone could be done for manslaughter. I wasn't sane at that moment . . . or actually, I think I was the most sane I'd ever been! And I slashed my wrists.

Then blood was spraying everywhere but I managed to do first aid on myself and shouted at Robert to call for an ambulance. I remember he said on the phone: 'Don't put the siren on, we don't want a scandal.' And in those days you went into hospital, they patched you up – I had four hours of microsurgery – and put you on a suicide watch ward. I remember I was with a nun who'd taken an overdose and another girl who'd taken an overdose of malaria pills, quinine, and had liver function problems. And they stuck you in the ward and, after they said: 'You may never get the use of your left arm again', it was bye-bye, and back to the same house, jammed full of – addicted to – Pethidine. And I knew as soon as I got back to the house and I couldn't open this can of tomato soup, and Rob said: 'No, you will have oxtail', I knew that nothing had changed and I had to escape. I remember standing there looking at the Pethidine, just thinking: 'I could just take all of those and this will be over', and then I thought: 'No, I've got to get away', and phoned up a removal van. The guy came along and I just threw everything into plastic bags, because I knew Robert wouldn't create a scene, and, with friends' help, I kind of disappeared. I just sort of ran away.

★★★

So that was really my first big breakdown and nothing was done about it, so coming up to the next one in 1994, did I realise what was going on? No! I'd been working in television for some years by then – I was a TV presenter and also running my own production company – and I'd got talked into yet another unsuitable relationship and had two children. I had Billie at nearly thirty-two and Billie was my first love . . . I remember having Billie, breastfeeding Billie, and I think that was the first time I felt connected to the planet and it was not what I expected. So I had Billie and basically my second husband Mark, I'm not saying he didn't love Billie, he did, but he was also a daily dope smoker, as was I. And I suddenly said: 'Right, no more drugs! I'm going to be mother of the year.' I went everywhere with Billie in the backpack but Mark wasn't as one-track as me, so there was that polarisation, but I absolutely decided I was going to get pregnant again, and did, with my daughter Madi.

Now, with the benefit of hindsight, I can see that Mark was very angry about a lot of things but didn't vocalise it and his way of dealing with it was to have an affair. She was a researcher who worked for my production company, a person who I didn't particularly like or dislike, but someone who I'd given a chance, training her up, and she'd come to me with all her boyfriend problems. Little did I realise she'd finished with him long ago so I was saying: 'I know what you're going through', when of course I didn't! She was talking about my husband and screwing around with my head. Then, when I found out about the betrayal . . . I always say if he'd had an affair with somebody I didn't know it wouldn't have been as bad, but finding out that he'd had an affair with somebody I'd taken under my wing, it's the classic: 'Fuck you, I'll show you: bang, bang!'

So if you take everything together: I had my own production company, I was working like a maniac, I was the main breadwinner, my husband was having an affair, and my new baby Madi had nearly died so I'd been up four days and nights with her. So there was nothing, I had nothing, in the reserve tank. I wasn't sleeping, my head was just going 'zuh, zuh, zuh' – skidding I call it because it's like a wheel skidding – with thoughts that jump, and go over and over again, and become faster and faster, and you become more and more awake. And I'd wake up at 3.30 in the morning like that. So it almost felt as if the day started at 3.30 and then, you know, it was like: 'Where does night end and where does . . . ?' It just all blurred, it joined up, not even really realising what day of the week it was, or anything like that.

Typically, at that time, I would skip breakfast because I was freaking out in the morning, I was just so jittery. It was like being on speed really. I remember when I was an air stewardess, we all used to take slimming tablets – this was in the '80s, way before we knew what they were – because we were always on the fatties list. And that was the same thing: like this wide-eyed, jittery, grinding teeth, jaw ache, thirsty, too cold, too hot, too this, too that. Then I started getting all obsessive about my eating again. And then I started thinking, when I went power walking, that I had to get to the next corner before the next car or the kids would die. You know, it just all started again. Did I equate all that to when I was fourteen? No! It was only later, in therapy, when I was made to look back, that you start seeing the patterns, but when you're in the middle of it, you don't recognise it.

I didn't want to be dead. I just wanted the noise, the crap, the everything, to stop, you know? My daughter had nearly died as an infant, meanwhile the husband's having the affair, then I find out that. I just wanted him to stop shouting at me and calling me this, that, and the other. Then the bank manager would get on the phone and say he's taken all the money out of the account. And then there's work and I just, you know, I wanted the shit to stop. So I overdosed with pills and alcohol. Then I rang my friend Dr Rosie King, who used to co-present the show *Live It Up* with me, because I thought: 'Ah . . . the kids.' Not me. Then I vaguely remember going into Northside, a psychiatric hospital, and when I realised I was still alive, I remember I think I said: 'Oh crap.' Because it meant the shit hadn't stopped. And when it hadn't stopped, I didn't think: 'Oh, I'm still alive', it was: 'Oh, I'm still here'. And the world doesn't change cos you've done something, although you have some hope that it will.

You very quickly learn in a psych hospital that nothing you do is normal. If you swore – you said 'fuck' – it was: 'Aggressive behaviour.' When I got cross it was: 'Ohhh, patient angry.' If you laughed: 'Inappropriate.' And that's the thing, when you're admitted to hospital, you're just a mental illness, nobody knows what your personality is, do they? Everything's mad: if you've got a filthy sense of humour, it's madness. Then they came round every fifteen minutes at night and shone a torch in your face to see if you were sleeping, so you wake up and then you get reported for having interrupted sleep. And then I had my ex-husband coming in, well my estranged husband coming in, and shouting at me and I'd get angry and upset and they'd just sit there and let it happen. And then it was written up as: 'I understand you became very agitated . . .'. No, I had someone there going: 'You're a nutter, you're a psycho, I'm going to get the kids off you.' So I'd lose my temper, you know?

Then there were psychiatrists asking questions – 'How do you feel today on a scale of one to four?' – and a trainee psychiatrist who was a bloody idiot. He came along and he said:

'Oh, so you have sexual problems.'

'Why?'

'Because you're wearing two bras.'

'No I'm not, it's a nursing bra.'

Then, when they gave me a medical:

'I see you've tried to stab your stomach.'

'No, that's a linear nigra, cos I've just had a baby.'

So I just thought: 'Right, I'm never talking to you ever again.' Which I didn't.

So then I was, like: 'I won't do anything, I'll just sit there like this.'

And that's what I really remember first and foremost about Northside – that I decided that if I sat very still in one place no one would notice me. I just thought: 'If I sit really still, really quietly, and I don't have eye contact, then I won't be here, they can't get to me.' You know when two year olds cover their eyes and they think they disappear? It was like that.

The only person who got through to me at the time was this one nurse Elaine, cos she treated me like a human being. She fought for Madi to come to the hospital so I could breastfeed her, and with Billie playing, and breastfeeding Madi, that was my solace and Elaine worked that out. I remember that the skin contact of just holding Madi was so precious, and her face and her eyes . . . she didn't look at me like I was mad, she looked at me like mummy. At first they had the door open with some nurse sitting there watching me, you know, in case I was a danger to my children. And I was so ashamed . . . I couldn't understand why they thought I might harm them. But Elaine really read it and I remember her coming past and saying: 'I don't think we need this door open', and kicking the doorstop.

I remember I had a TV in my room and Elaine would just come and lean up in the doorway and watch TV. Not sit, not trying to be my friend, just stand. And I'll never forget I was watching Billy Connolly do his bike ride through Scotland and I used to love going to Scotland as a child. When we were on holiday the parents would . . . I don't know what they'd do, they'd just leave us to it. So we'd go to the ice-skating centre or just camp by the loch and sing and make our voices echo, so I had really fond memories of Scotland. So I remember watching that and she just used to make odd comments about Billy Connolly – not looking at me, just using the TV – and it was really clever of her. And gradually I'd sort of say something like: 'Been there.' And really she was the one who did more than all the psychiatrists. I learnt a lot from the way she treated me in that hospital.

At first, nobody in the business knew where I was, I just lied to everybody. I hadn't even told my publicist what was going on, I'd just said I was taking some time off. This was despite the fact that I'd been on the public record talking about mental health – and working in mental health – since the late '80s, after my sister Linda, who had schizophrenia, killed herself. At the time I was advised to just say that she had 'died of an illness' but I'd had enough of hiding it like a dirty secret, so I told it like it was: the stigma, the effect on the family, her suffering, everything. And you know what? I got a really positive response and a lot of people – both the public and well-known people – came out and said: 'I'm glad you talked about it.' And then the Minister of Health in Australia asked me to chair the National Community Advisory Group on Mental Health, which I jumped at and did for ten years, alongside my media career. So up until the point of my breakdown I'd been saying: 'If only people with mental health problems would stand up and be counted!' And then, you know, when it came to me it was like: 'Screw that! All you other people, you stand up and be counted!'

But then, after a few weeks at Northside, there was a phone call – the nurses said: 'There's a phone call for you' – and I went to the phone and it was this journalist saying: 'Oh, so you *are* at Northside Clinic, yes we heard.' And I freaked. I was freaking out anyway at that time – you know, I couldn't even look at the leaves on the trees out the window, I didn't like the way they moved, let alone dealing with something like this. So I got really upset, really agitated, and I was ashamed. Because I was a journalist myself, I just knew it wouldn't be honest, it would be sensationalised. I could have written the bloody headlines: 'Nutter' and/or 'Suicide bid'. And then you get everyone going: 'How selfish! These people! Don't they think of their families? How selfish!' And I remember ringing my publicist up and talking to her, crying, saying: 'I'm in Northside. What are we going to do?'

So she came and signed me out for the afternoon, collected me – because I virtually couldn't walk – and took me to her house. And we sat down and she said: 'We'll do this in our own words, we'll kill it.' And that's been my thing ever since: 'I'll kill it first.' So anyway, we did the story with this journalist we knew, in a woman's magazine, and they had the exclusive, and I was allowed to sit down and go through it all, which was unheard of in those days. But they had a scoop and the story was, you know, it was as good as it could be, it was really good. And the public reaction was okay actually. It helped that I handled it my way: the way I talked about it and explained it just normalised it, and a lot of other people could say: 'Yeah, I've felt like that.' It wasn't just done in sound bites and sensational headlines so the general public, en masse, was less scary.

Having said that, after I came out of hospital none of the good old journos I knew could meet my eye. Nobody talked about it, it was never mentioned, it was like it never happened. It was only when I went back to the first mental health group meeting that I felt really okay with everybody. I remember one of them said: 'We'd just like to welcome you back and tell you how great it is that you'll now be able to hear exactly the same voices we can!' We had all these in-jokes that only we could understand, and they were really great.

***

When I got the call from England out of the blue to come and do the chat show, *Trisha*, in 1998, I hadn't worked in television for . . . oh, several years. After coming out of Northside, me and Mark divorced and I gave up nearly all my media work to concentrate on really just getting better, bonding with my daughters, and doing voluntary mental health work. During that time I also met my husband Peter, while interviewing him for a government job in mental health, and we'd only been married a matter of months when the job offer came in, so I left the final decision to him. And even though he had a great career in Australia, he told me it was an amazing opportunity and to go for it. So I accepted the job, having told them everything – the breakdown, the panic attacks, the depression, everything – and insisted on having lots of rest time written into my contract so I could concentrate on my family and not be so career-driven. I'd come to recognise some of my patterns by then – through therapy, which I'll come back to – and there was no way I was going back to how I was.

The only problem was that I was taking quite a lot of anti-depressants by this time, which I wouldn't have at Northside – I refused, I refused – as I was breastfeeding. I was on . . . oh God, what was I on? I can't remember now, my memory's crap. But I didn't want to be on antidepressants when I came to do the

job so I came off them in a matter of weeks, really quickly, and
it was . . . urgh. I was saying to someone the other day, it was
the *worst* experience, the *worst*, I didn't know anything could
be so *bad*. And I'm not a wimp – I had two children, no pain
killers, no nothing, I can do pain like no one else, I zone out.
But man, that was bad. They didn't tell me, they said, you
know: 'There may be side effects', but whoa.

The things that stand out in my mind? I was chairing a mental health group for service users and carers and we all met
at this hotel at Sydney Airport because people had to fly in
from whatever country. And it had this big sweeping open slat
staircase in the middle and I was talking to a dear friend, Judy,
and we're walking down the stairs, and I couldn't judge where
the next step was. And I was halfway down, or a third of the
way down, the first flight – cos there was a flight, and then a
flat bit, and then more – and I just remember thinking: 'How
the bloody hell am I going to get down?' I was in the middle, I
couldn't even hold on, and I was, like: 'Woah.' And the terror
. . . I was like: 'Judy, I can't.' I said: 'Judy, Judy, get me . . .' and
she got me to the rail and it was literally like holding on and
going step by step. Then I sat there and had some water and I
said: 'I'll be alright, I'll be alright', like an idiot.

I remember I had a little Kia Sportage and I drove from the
airport and it was horrific. All the traffic from the different ter-
minals converge and there's this one place, this roundabout, and
it's like: 'Go to this turn, go to that turn', and I got this tingling
in my mouth and then I thought: 'I can't read, I can't read.'
And then I thought: 'I can't even see', I couldn't understand
the lanes. And in Australia we always had automatic cars and I
just thought: 'I can't drive.' It was a complete cold, confused
panic. Now I'd had panic attacks before – with the breathing
and all that – but you know they're coming because there's that
build-up, you know? And I remember just thinking: 'Jesus',

and putting my hazard lights on and sitting there and people beeping at first and then thinking I'd broken down. And then I was thinking: 'Well, what do I do?' Because if it was panicking I'd breathe but I remember trying to do all my breathing exercises and nothing. Then, after about ten, fifteen minutes, it sort of went and I remember crawling, just thinking: 'Is it going to come back again?' And it didn't, but that's what it would do.

So coming off the pills was just . . . just horrific. If I hadn't had Peter and I didn't want to be off the antidepressants because of the job, I'd totally understand people saying: 'Well, you know what, I'll just stay on them.' You know, I can absolutely understand that, because *boy*. Being on them was fine, I just felt whatever normal is, but coming off them was just God awful, really awful. It was so bad that I didn't think I'd be able to cope with going to England and doing the show but, with support from my therapist and Peter, I did it.

★★★

I've said it before but that's cos it's true: since 1998, when I married Peter and moved to England to start the *Trisha* show, I feel like my life's been blessed. Before, I was totally career driven, went from bad relationship to bad relationship, and had no support. Bugger all! Nothing! But now, well, my family understand. I am married to someone who's at the top of their field: Peter's not only a psychotherapist, he lectures and trains other psychotherapists, so blimey. Then there's my daughters. My younger daughter's done mental health first aid – she's one of the youngest people in the country to have done it – and she's worked in her summer holidays in a halfway type house, and both my daughters have worked at Mind on a voluntary basis. So I've got a family around me who are very aware of mental health issues and aren't frightened to flag those up.

It's so different to when I think about growing up with my half-sister, Linda, who had schizophrenia. If the rellies came over, and she was off her face on Largactil at the hospital, they'd race up there and get her out and then mum would make a joke about teenagers out on the town, you know: 'Ooh, she's got a hangover.' It was all secret, secret, secret. Even though they worked as psych nurses, it was always: 'No one must know.' So the beauty of my family now is that all of us are allowed to bring it up and talk about habits and situations and behaviours that might be worrying us. So there's this complete contrast from growing up in the '60s and '70s in terms of understanding and support.

Another huge part of my recovery process has been talking therapies. I first started them in 1994 because, in order to get out of Northside, I'd had to agree to have six months of therapy. I *had* to sign up for that. So I started seeing a psychotherapist up to three times a week at first and then, after the six months, when I could have given up, I carried on until I left for England because I found it really helpful. I also had relaxation therapy, which I thought was bullshit and wouldn't work, but I remember once this woman did this session with me, with all these sea noises and imagining this, and that, and the other. And she said: 'There, how do you feel?' and I said: 'Yeah, great nap, thank you for that', and she said: 'You weren't sleeping at all, you were awake the whole way through.' And that's the first time I thought: 'Ohh, maybe it's not bullshit.'

I then went back into therapy in about 2005/6, after mum died and my stepdad went to my husband and said: 'Has Trisha ever had any issues about her, er, identity or parentage or childhood?' And Peter said: 'Er, just a bit!' And he said: 'Ah, alright, why?' And he said: 'Well, she doesn't feel she fits in and blah, blah, blah, blah, blah.' And he said: 'Well, I'm not her dad.' I'd known from the word go really, you know, but it just brought up so much stuff that I said to Peter: 'I need to go into therapy', because I now do things to safeguard myself against becoming ill. So I saw this chap, John, who's a psychotherapist who works a lot with children, which was really, really good for me. Everybody talks about the here and now but with John he almost, not treated me as a child, but because he'd worked with children so much – it sounds corny – but he could talk to the child within me. Because there *was* this child, there was arrested development. Oh, I wonder why?! So there was a part of me that was very vulnerable and very scared and he took me really, really back. Things like phobias and fears I had, he was: 'Right, let's look at that.'

Because CBT's good at how to manage things but there's a risk of it coming back if you don't . . . well, it depends what sort of person you are. I like to understand things. I can deal with things if I can deconstruct them and understand them because I have that sort of analytical mind. If somebody says: 'Just do this, this, this and this', never mind about the why, I'm like: 'Well, I'll give it a go, but . . .'. But when you can understand how those things came about, for one thing you stop beating yourself up. So the talking therapies made me realise where this fear of lack of control, and disordered eating, and ritualised depression, came from. It was my way of trying to survive and it had outlived its purpose.

So for me, and it's different for everyone, the most important part of my recovery process was understanding and forgiving, forgiving myself. Because the thing about mental illness, partly because of the way society looks at it, is that you spend so much time and energy – you don't even realise you're doing it – being angry with yourself for being like that. You know, a lot of people take on a victimised persona and that's a form of anger. That: 'I can't help it', that absolute helplessness. I wasn't one of those people, I never felt a victim, I was like: 'Argh,

why am I like this?' But that victimisation – that inverted form
of anger, of frustration – saps the hell out of you. I think once
you can forgive yourself and understand why you became that
way, and it doesn't matter why – could be brain chemistry,
childhood, coping – for me, that was important. And saying:
'You know what? You're not that mad or bad or stupid. You
survived.'

You're only as much of a victim as you make yourself. Any
illness – I don't care if it's physical, mental, whatever – any
illness requires putting some part of yourself into getting well.
And that's not a bad thing, it's a good thing, because you take
back some control, no matter how small. You just need to get
your nail underneath and worry that bit of control because
that's the first step. And it's the little things, not the big grand
things. It can be: 'Right, today I'm going to go up and down
the stairs twenty times – even if I have to miss the fourth step!'
That can be a start; having a small goal is good. Like, even if
you have to write down what you're going to eat and when
you're going to eat it, which I remember doing and sticking on
the wall. Or, you know, a mood chart – brilliant – get a big old
calendar, or make one, and use gummy stars or just a felt pen
and chart shit days. At the end of the day: 'How was today?'
And for every bad thing, you put a blue star. And then you
ask: 'What was a good thing?' Because then you start seeing if
your moods follow a pattern. And it helps you to recognise that
there's dark and shade, there's light and shade.

It's about, as I say, getting that fingernail under reality and
stripping reality right back down to all those tiny things which
help connect you. So get a pet, look after the pet. Get a plant,
a pot plant. Mad things, but they work. Sensory things are
good. I did quilting for a long time, with lots of different scraps
of material, which I had to go and choose. I didn't want to go
out, I hated going out, but I had to choose the scraps, so I had

a reason. And I could feel the scraps and I had to hand sew them, so I felt the rough bits and the silky bits. It's a bit like food. I make sure that I have lots of different textures of food and I make myself stop and think about it. And I always have flowers around the house for the smell, so I can go and just close my eyes and smell. Again, it's a sensory thing, because my issue is disconnecting from things, so feel and smell are important. Or if you've got a camera on your phone, start taking photographs. Even if they're stupid ones, like I did yesterday . . . I took one of a poppy, a red poppy in this field of white peas, just one on its own. And it's not a great picture, it was a bit blurred, but for me it's more about what it repres- sents. I thought: 'Ah, this is different, that proves you can be different.' The beauty in difference. So things like that – it's a bit like food for the mind.

For me, running is also really important, although I don't think of it as exercise. I need it because I naturally have a lot of energy, I'm really bad sitting in one place and doing nothing. It probably is obsessive, but that's another thing I recognise: that I *am* obsessive, so I look for good obsessions, or helpful obsessions, or diverting obsessions. I think it's my way of cop- ing. I don't think: 'Right, you've got an obsession so get rid of those', or 'You've got panic or anxiety, get rid of those.' These things were developed in me. I created them in me – added with brain chemistry and childhood and all the rest of it – as a way of protecting myself, so they're not all bad. So I'm going to look for what I can get, you know, what I can do, that's utilising that.

I think as an adult if you come to be treated, or helped, with a mental health problem, it's very hard for someone to say: 'Right, I know this is how you've been operating for the past thirty-five years or forty years but bugger that, we're going to start again.' I think it would help to say: 'Right, you're really good at being obsessive about something so what can we do? Let's see, what if you were to walk every day? And where's a really good place? Okay, if cracks in the pavement are a problem, we'll do cross country.' And that's what I do, cross country, so I don't get obsessive about traffic, and green's really calming. So I haven't had to ditch all those protective elements of my mental health problem so I feel a lot more secure, I don't feel stripped of who I am. It's important that we don't just see it as: 'That's mental illness.' Because where do I end and where does the mental illness start? It's better to see it as: 'You've got some good qualities in this mental illness and let's use them to help you live a more productive and happier life.'

I think the other thing that's really helped me is being allowed to incorporate my spirituality, because that was never allowed and it's not readily accepted within a mental health system. But it was actually one of the things I went to when I was fourteen, because I was dealing with death and darkness and destruction, and at fourteen the only thing that could save me – that anybody had as a way of being saved – was stuff that was in the Bible. Because you were told: 'And the Lord said I will save you', and: 'You walk through the valley of death.' I remember reading *Pilgrim's Progress*. The only thing on the horizon, where anyone was talking about getting you out of hell, and describing the kind of hell that I was in, was faith. You know? And I guess, as a child myself, through schoolwork and this idea of a faith, and a God – something bigger – that was my lifeline. If I was going to be anything now I'd be a Bahá'í – because I believe all faiths are the same – but now my church is really outside: the green. I need the green, the trees, I love being out, and I love being with my dog, Alf.

Also, I think it's so important to recognise the child within you and to play. Like yesterday, it was really muddy and I was skipping and Peter's saying: 'Those people are laughing at you', and I don't care, I think it's okay to be that child. And both my girls play, we play a lot, we play every day. They'll say something to me and I'll sing: *'Today, I'm in an opera, we're going to sing!'* But you're not allowed to be like that when you're with grown-ups . . . well, with some grown-ups you can, but a lot of them you can't. I think a lot of people struggle to do that, especially in my industry. In order to lose control they have to get pissed and act stupid, and I think that's really mentally unhealthy. Whereas I've seen it's really important for me to include it as part of my day: to be absolutely stone-cold sober and enjoy it and have that sense of relief, of laughing, and being silly and frivolous. Again, it sounds corny, but there is a child inside and I need to embrace it, allow it, enjoy it. It is very, very therapeutic.

★★★

Have I ever faced stigma? No, I don't think so, not personally. You're allowed to have a mental health problem and be a celebrity: it's almost *de rigueur*, isn't it? You know, it's like: 'Oh good, another one!' It's like artist and mad, sort of thing. I think the 'risk', in inverted commas, is facing stigma because of the people who you advocate for or support. So while celebrities might be allowed to have those eccentricities, I don't kid myself, because I see how it is with the advocates and people I work with, with refugees and how they're treated. So I'm under no illusions. There's no glamour in being a mental health patron – with mental health they think it's catching and they still connect mad and bad. Where are the big balls to do with mental health? Who are the glitzy stars who hold star-spangled do's for mental health? You know, there's no glitz, there's no glamour, no pink or red ribbons, no Liz Hurleys and Elton Johns.

When I had breast cancer everyone was my best friend, wanting to come and hug me and saying: 'Can you do this, and can you do that, and can you be guest of honour at this, that, and the other?' Oh, I could live high on being a spokesperson for a breast cancer charity, which I will not be. There's far more glamour in that than in mental health. See, breast cancer is a disease of mothers and we all know mothers are saints: you know, the martyr. And to be honest, when you're going through it, because the mum is usually the core of the family, mum going down is awful. But mum being mad, it's: 'Bad mother', or mum being suicidal it's: 'What about the children? She should have the children taken away from her.' You know, I remember saying to someone: 'Imagine being diagnosed with breast cancer and someone comes along and says, 'I think we might have to get social services involved, we might have to take your child away.' But that's regularly the suggestion with mental health, in headlines and in reality.

So, yeah, how's it impacted on my life? Bad and good. At the end of the day, it *is* my life, it's shaped my life. It's who I am. So I live with it, I manage it, in the same way as someone who's prone to high cholesterol, or someone with asthma, or someone with diabetes. The decisions you make day to day, and in the long run, decide whether you suffer from those conditions or you live with those conditions, and I live with them and they have upsides and they have downsides. If you've had something since you're fourteen, it is part of who you are and that's . . . it's not a bad thing.

CHARLES WALKER

Member of Parliament, Conservative

'At OCD's most spiteful, you're blackmailed; a hundred blackmails a day. It has ranges of blackmails, but at its most spiteful, if you don't do a particular thing then someone you really do love is going to die. And you know that that is total nonsense – that's the weird thing, you have total insight – you know it's completely, completely crazy, but you're not going to risk it.'

Born in 1967, Charles Walker was educated at the American School in London, followed by the University of Oregon, where he studied Political Science. On his return to the UK, he worked in numerous marketing and communications roles and became involved in local politics. Charles was the parliamentary candidate for Ealing North in the 2001 general election and was elected to the House of Commons in 2005 as the Conservative member for Broxbourne. Stepson of former Conservative MP and middle-distance runner Christopher Chataway, Charles lives with his wife Fiona and their three children, Charlotte, Alistair, and James, in Goffs Oak. Charles has suffered from obsessive compulsive disorder (OCD), a type of anxiety disorder, since childhood, and has used this personal

experience to campaign widely on mental health issues as a politician. The interview for this chapter took place at his office,
just days after he 'came out' as suffering from OCD in the House
of Commons debate on mental health in June 2012, in which
he memorably referred to himself as a 'practising fruitcake'.

***

Come in, come in. Right. Good. Over the last two weeks, ten
days, I can tell you I've talked about this a fair bit. It's quite
interesting: you get the news coverage first – it becomes a news
story – then it becomes a features story, and then you get the
academics. Does that . . . ? That seems to be the way it works,
or is working. So, anyway, fire away.

When was I diagnosed with OCD? I wasn't. I still haven't
had an official diagnosis, I self-diagnosed. I know I've got it.
Although I only worked out that it was OCD probably in
recent years, to be honest. Looking back now though, I say
that I was thirteen when I was first 'visited by OCD', when
it came onto my shoulder for the first time. I was at St John's
Wood tube station buying a ticket and I was convinced that the
person selling me the ticket could hear what I was thinking.
And of course, at age thirteen you don't know that's OCD,
but then it started to manifest itself in the usual sort of ways:
not treading on lines, having to touch things multiple times,
counting, coming in and out of rooms, light switches. And
then there were the voices of self-doubt, although they're not
audible voices – you're worried that you've said something
inappropriate, you're worried about how people are going to
react – and all this is part of OCD.

So that's how it manifested itself pretty much from day one
and, you know, it was difficult. Thirteen is a difficult age, and
I remember it as a very difficult time, particularly as I moved

school that year. Having said that, my stepsister sent me a text yesterday saying: 'I beg to differ with your analysis about when you got OCD.' She said: 'I remember you as a child aged five and you wouldn't go to bed until everything was organised just right in the bathroom.' Which is interesting and I don't recall that. But it makes sense as my parents divorced when I was young and from the age of three to six there were tough times and I felt I wasn't in control of my environment. And OCD is all about controlling events – my view of OCD is that it's about finding balance, feeling that *you're* in control. The problem is, the more you feed it, the more *it's* in control. Yep?

It can almost torment you to a degree where everything you're doing, everything, takes so long, as the rituals just become more pronounced and more demanding. I'm particularly bad in the kitchen so – when I'm really being very tedious – I'll walk through the door, go to the fridge and get a diet coke, so you've got to wash your hands because you've been in the fridge. You'll get something out of the bread bin, wash your hands. You'll get some salt out of the cupboard, wash your hands. You'll put the Diet Coke can in the recycling bin, wash your hands. Do you see what I mean? And I know, from people who have contacted me, that I'm not at the desperate end of the spectrum, nowhere near the desperate end of the spectrum. Some people are constantly washing their hands because of germs – they're terrified – but it's just routine, you've got to wash your hands so many times. So it really can dominate your life. Getting out the bath can take an extra five or ten minutes. Oh, it's like . . . God, getting out of the garden can take an extra five or ten minutes. You know? Grrr.

I operate to the rule of four, so I have to do everything in evens. So if I'm walking the dog and it's snowed, for example, then if I touch the snow once to feel the texture – I love climates and snow – then I have to touch it two times, then two times with that hand, then another two times, and another two times. Or when I go to the loft I have to switch the light on four times, you know? Again, the bathroom, I have to wash my hands four times. It's no laugh when you've washed your hands repeatedly, and you don't dry them because you're so pissed off, and then you press a light switch and get a shock. Another thing I do is I have to walk in and out of the room four times. I mean, I don't want to be rude to Michael Flatley, but I said I look like an extra from *Riverdance*, coming in and out of a room, so my family call it the 'Michael Flatley's'. You know, all the: 'Diddly, diddly'. So they say: 'Dad's got the Michael Flatley's again.' So my wife and children often make light of it – often it's: 'Come on Dad, get on with it!' – which is helpful because I think you don't want to make an issue out of it.

Although sometimes, very occasionally, when it really does kick you in the head, I'll say to my wife: 'That was a bad day', and she'll say: 'I know it was bad because your rituals have been bad.' You know, she can spot it, I don't need to tell her now that I've had a bad, or even a bloody nightmare, day. And she's been an absolute hero to bear with it. I'm lucky I've got a very patient wife, because I think I have been quite demanding. I think Mrs Walker – if she was to be frank with me – would probably admit that it's been a bigger pain in the arse for her than I ever thought it was, because I have a *level* of insight, but you're never quite sure how difficult you are. I can be quite awkward because I can obsess on things. I could be up for hours looking for an interest rate statement from a bank account two years ago that might only be for £7.50 and which actually I don't really need. But it's about control. So occasionally Mrs Walker will say: 'You are being bloody difficult at the moment.' So when it's bad, I'm given a fairly wide berth . . . no, that's not right. I'm given a lot of latitude and slack. Latitude and slack, that's what I mean, and that's why I'm lucky.

I mean, I've read stories where it just destroys marriages, it destroys relationships, it really does hurt and damage families. It can become a monster, I mean, a monster. As many people have said to me, it's like an unwelcome house guest – as is any mental illness – that can, at times, grind you down and make you feel very unhappy. It drives people just . . . it can drive people round the bend; it drives me round the bend at times. I've had it at times where I've felt very depressed and miserable. I'd describe it as malevolent – it's malevolent – God, is it a destructive illness. Although is it an illness? It's a mental . . . it's mental ill health. I think we need to redefine mental illness; it's mental ill health. Do you see what I mean? Mental ill health is more DEFCON 3 than DEFCON 2. Does that make sense?

Having said that, people do tend to trivialise OCD, so they think it's all about putting your pencils in a line. And maybe the person who does that does have OCD, but there are grades of OCD. At OCD's most spiteful, you're blackmailed; a hundred blackmails a day. It has ranges of blackmails, but at its most spiteful, if you don't do a particular thing then someone you really do love is going to die. And you know that that is total nonsense – that's the weird thing, you have total insight – you know it's completely, completely crazy, but you're not going to risk it. I was on holiday recently and I took a beautiful photograph of my son carrying a fishing rod and I was glowing with pride, but then the voice started: 'If you don't get rid of that photograph, your child will die.' You fight those voices for a couple or three hours and you know that you really should not give into them because they should not be there and it ain't going to happen. But, in the end, you ain't going to risk your child, so one gives into the voices and then feels pretty miserable about life afterwards.

So in my view, OCD is when it actually really starts to impact upon your happiness and welfare and well-being. It's when, after six months, you haven't been able to move on – when it actually starts to impact upon your medium- to long-term happiness and equilibrium. That's when perhaps you need to start thinking: 'Look, there's no reason I should sit around feeling miserable, maybe I should go and talk to someone about it or sort it out.' Although I haven't, I haven't. Listen, we're going to have a really disappointing interview on this, because I haven't. Because, you know, I'm a typical man. I know that you can do cognitive behavioural therapy, you can take antidepressants, so I know that there *are* treatments out there and maybe I will go out and embrace them. But no, I haven't so far. It's a male thing isn't it? Personally, I wouldn't want to take drugs, but I want to make it clear that I've nothing against them and that there's lots of people they work very, very, well for.

And really I would say that for the last four and a half years it's been pretty benign for me. There have been moments, there have been periods of anxiety in there where it flairs up, but they've been short periods. So it's not been tricky for me for the last few years and I think that's because I'm more settled in what I'm doing. I mean today, for instance, I've washed my hands a few times – at times when you'd expect me to wash my hands, to be honest, like before a meal – and I'll always take a bit longer because I have to do that, that, that and that, but it's not very active at the moment.

***

If you were to ask me: 'When were the most active times of your OCD?' it would be the times when I was most anxious and I imagine most professionals in this field, and I'm not a professional, would say that makes perfect sense. The problem is, it comes at times when I'm very stressed, so, let's think: going to a new school when I was thirteen, going to university, first job, changing jobs, losing (which I was always going to do) the general election in 2001 and not having a job to go to after that, getting selected for parliament. So it's periods of great change and uncertainty which trigger anxiety. I mean, it was very bad after I was elected to the House of Commons, then it plateaued, but then you get spikes. So during the expenses scandal, for example, when you were totally out of control – you didn't know whether you'd done anything wrong or whether you were going to – it was just totally off the scale. Because you're trying to find control, you're trying to find balance. Does that make sense? So that would be an example where it wasn't good. And nobody would be sympathetic, and I wouldn't ask for it, the last thing I want is any sympathy.

When I first got into parliament in 2005 it was extraordinary. Nothing prepares you for being in the public eye. You think you want to be an MP, I was selected, and within two days the OCD came roaring back and it lasted for two years. It was the scrutiny – or the sense of scrutiny, even if it's not happening you imagine it's there – the expectation, the directness with which people communicate with you. It's a complete sensory overload and I don't think anything prepares you for that. Suddenly, you know, you're reading the newspaper and there's a journalist calling you a fat Tory – not that that would worry me in the slightest now – but it's part of the jigsaw. So I think a lot of colleagues struggle in their first two years, I really do, I think that's pretty factual, because you come into politics and it's a hostile world. Your motives are always questioned and you very quickly realise that it doesn't matter that you're a new broom. In a sense the media treat you as before and constituents will be very direct with you – often very warm but sometimes very direct – so I think the first two years are difficult in this place for anyone.

The House of Commons is very good for finding a weakness.

If you've got a weakness for drink, the House of Commons will find it – less so now because the hours have changed – but if you've got an addiction, in whatever way, it will find it. If you have a predilection for unhealthy eating, or eating too much, you know, it'll just find it. So if you have a weakness – and I don't want to say mental health is a weakness – but if you have something that you're struggling with, or prone to, I think the pressure of politics will aggravate it. It may have always been there but it will bring it to the fore. Because people are anxious here, so they might comfort eat, or smoke too much, or drink too much, or feel lonely and get themselves tangled up in situations that may well have happened in a marriage but perhaps they just get there earlier. I hope that makes sense.

And all the time you feel you're having to try to hide these things from everybody. And I'm very good at hiding it at work, but then you'll get home and it sort of explodes. Do you see what I mean? You can contain it but then it seems to go off the scale. Before talking about it publicly, I'd been involved in parliament for seven years and talked quite passionately about mental health, often without notes, or with very few notes, and people had occasionally said: 'Do you have personal experience?' And I'd say: 'Oh no, no, no, family experience, family experience.' But in the few years prior to that debate I was beginning to be less guarded in my conversations, I think I was just preparing, you know? I couldn't be bothered anymore. Afterwards, my wife was asked by a journalist: 'Did you know he was going to do it?' And she said: 'For the last three years he's been thinking about it.'

Because sometimes, with OCD, you just want to go to the top of a hill and just scream: 'Argh, argh!' Yeah? Well, when I stood up in the Commons and came out in that debate in June 2012 that was the equivalent: it was metaphorically just getting it off my chest. Brilliant. Let me tell you, having told the world about it, I feel 100 per cent better. I'm delighted to be out, delighted. It's about crossing that hurdle, saying: 'Listen, I suffer in a minor way, and have suffered in a minor way, and people just need to know that.' Because, you know, if everybody knows, it's not a problem. What can I say new on this? Well, in *Crocodile Dundee* when the journalist – I don't know what her name was – says:

'So what do you do when you've got a problem here Mick?'

Mick Dundee: 'I tell Wally.'

'And what does Wally do?'

'He tells everybody else and it's not a problem.'

Hooray! You know, genius!

It meant I could move on and how fantastic is that? I'm so privileged in a sense to have had the chance for self-therapy and that really was a great moment for me personally. I don't want to say it was self-indulgent – because it wasn't – but it was good for me, it was important for me. I hope other people felt that way, because it wasn't just me, there was a real sort of 'get it off your chest' feeling that day. And none of those colleagues were asking anybody to feel sorry for them, there was not an ounce of self-pity. And these are all people who, I think, politics is so much better for having them there. You know, we're constantly told that MPs are out of touch, that they don't have real life experiences and this, that, and the other, and that's rubbish. I mean, rubbish. Most members of parliament are there for all the right reasons and are pretty good, decent, normal people.

I didn't know what to expect after I spoke out. I knew that every time I'd spoken on mental health previously, people had quietly come up to me from all quarters and put their hand on my arm or elbow, or had taken me aside, and said: 'Thank you so much for what you're doing because my son or my daughter, my husband, my wife, my partner, my uncle, you know, my mum or dad . . .'. Do you see what I mean? So I knew there was a demand out there, in its crudest terms, for politicians to address this problem. But I think a lot of people felt that because there was almost this radio silence, that it wasn't something they wanted to talk about. But look, there's 650 MPs, so is it really possible that out of 650 MPs, up until that debate, none had mental health problems? I mean, we know there are members of parliament that have had difficulties, but nobody would actually stand up and admit to it.

On this issue, I actually think the public were well ahead of politicians. I got lovely emails from people after the debate, just extraordinary. I have been desperately moved by the emails I have received from parents, partners, spouses, and people with OCD. I wish you could read them, there are lines in those emails which are totally inspirational. Like one person who wrote to me saying he's almost there and when his OCD sparks up he says: 'Just you behave yourself.' Do you know what I mean? Try saying that to yourself: 'Just you behave yourself.' There's lots of lovely stuff in there but perhaps the most lovely email was: 'Dear Charles, better a fruitcake than a plain old sponge.' Absolutely uplifting stuff, extraordinary stuff, just extraordinary, from all people, from those right at the top of their professions, from all walks of life. Fascinating.

I think, interestingly, the media were ready to move on as well, I think the appetite for moving on was there. I mean, the media have been remarkable. I think the national papers and the tabloids have thought: 'You know what, the penny's dropping. We have been improving in the way we've treated mental health in the last five years, but we've still not been great, we've been using fairly inappropriate headlines. And we thought our readers liked that, but actually our readers are laughing nervously along with us while, in fact, not liking it inside at all. It's actually making them feel rather uncomfortable.' Do you understand what I'm saying? So maybe the media is thinking: 'We might be out of step with our readership on this.'

Somebody said to me in an interview afterwards: 'Have you ever been discriminated against?' And I have no idea. I hope not, I hope not, but you don't know. If one were to leave parliament I think there are clauses in certain employment contracts that say you can be dismissed if you develop mental health problems, which I shall be looking at very, very closely. You know, that worries me, I don't like that. There *is* discrimination out there and there *is* prejudice and we're going to be addressing that. I mean, I have no special right not to be discriminated against – but why *would* you discriminate, wouldn't it be ridiculous? This isn't meant to sound pompous, but politically I think I've been a moderate success: I'm Vice Chairman of the 1922 Committee, I'm on the board of the Party, I'm competent on my feet speaking. And I've done all this with OCD. So what would have changed since I went public with it?

What I want people to understand is that there are lots of people out there doing great jobs who actually have problems that they can manage and get on with it. Or they may have problems that they can't manage but the outside world doesn't know that because they're doing . . . because they're working hard. In fact, I would probably say that if employers were to look closely, some of their most high-functioning, dedicated, focused staff probably have – or are more likely to have – a mental health problem than perhaps the middle of the pack performers. Basically because you might always be trying to compensate. Do you see what I mean? You might be more driven.

It's certainly made me a better member of parliament. It's definitely made me stronger, much stronger, and more resilient. Because, you know, when you've beaten yourself up constantly, and then other people beat you up, one can smile and say: 'Yeah, well, okay, tell me something that I haven't already said to myself ten times today.' It's also improved my ability to cut through the bullshit. It's made me more independent minded: I'm pretty unbiddable, I'm pretty unwhippable. If there's something I believe is wrong or I don't want to do it, then I'm invariably going to say it's wrong and not do it. As long as I don't hurt and upset people, that's good enough for me. And you know what? I'm pretty sure that's because for the past thirty-one years I've been constantly doing deals with myself, constantly negotiating a balance with this OCD. And so at the end of the day, there's part of my life – my professional life – where I'm not willing to compromise too much.

Does that make sense? It's a hard one this, I don't know how you're going to project this. Let's just try that one again. I'll tell you what, I'm so – happy's such a weak word – I'm so pleased and delighted and honoured to be a backbench member of parliament. It's been a struggle to get here at times and now that I *am* here I'm going to do the right thing for me – I don't ever want to betray myself and do something I don't believe in. And I'm sure that may be connected to OCD, you know? In a sense, you're already exhausted when you get here and you're like: 'Now I'm here, to hell with it, I'm going to do it the way I want to do it.' So it's probably made me truer to myself.

★★★

Now I think I've been given a gift. For thirty-one years I've had this unwelcome house guest that, at times, has made me feel very, very, very depressed and anxious. But at the end of the day – and this is where I make the point that I have a great life in so many ways – if actually this small hardship I've had to endure for thirty-one years has prepared me to campaign on mental health, as I've done in the last seven years, then in some ways it's a blessing. It's a blessing if it's put me in a position to do what I did along with other very brave members of parliament . . . no, very *useful* members of parliament, what we did wasn't *brave*, it was *useful*. Fighting for your country is brave, working at A&E is brave, being on the front line as a police officer in a riot is brave, what we did was useful. But if it allowed me to do that then actually maybe it *is* a blessing. Because I think in some ways OCD has shaped my personality, so actually, and I don't want to sound pompous – and I can always sound pompous when I'm trying not to – the lovely thing is that it's allowed me to pursue this interest in mental health.

It's allowed me to feel I've made a contribution, and we all want to make a contribution. When I became an MP some-body said to me: 'Oh, the Chamber of the House of Commons is a waste of time', you know: 'Nobody listens to what goes on in the Chamber. It's what we do outside the Chamber that counts.' You've seen this, you follow politics. 'Backbencher MPs, there's not really anything much you can get done.' And I said: 'Hmm, we'll see about that', and in a sense there's a slight ego thing here, to prove people wrong, to show that actually parliament matters. I have a blinding faith in politics to do good and that's what drives me. We are so lucky as members of parliament that we have this amazing place where, if you work hard, you can make a difference to an area as important as mental health.

And there is no magic solution to this but I think we need to get to a stage where people feel more able to get help. And help doesn't have to be pharmaceutical, help doesn't necessarily have to be professional, help could be a place where you can sit down with a group of people and have a chat. You know, we have Alcoholics Anonymous, so surely we could have some-thing where people could go when they're feeling a bit blue, a bit down, where they can go and chat with other people, some of whom have got much better. You know, this is a societal problem, as I said in my speech, and we just need to find ways of helping people confront their problems, talk about their problems, and cross back into mainstream society with people who can sort of shepherd them there and hold their hand in times of difficulty. It's not impossible. I'd love to see something like Alcoholics Anonymous around mental health.

I know that I'm lucky in that I've got a fantastic support network, I've got a job I love – a vocation, not a job, a vocation I love – a fantastic family, I'm comfortably off. So even when it's really bad, even when it's really, really bad, you kind of know it's going to get better. Does that make sense? That may not make you feel great but you sort of feel there is hope. What worries me are the people who don't have all the support networks around them – who are isolated, alone, financially stressed, living in a difficult environment. It must be very difficult for them; I feel greatly for them because then it must just be dreadful. You know, possibly each day worse than the one before. It must be so desperately lonely and perhaps frightening . . . no, definitely frightening. So that is something that worries me greatly, it really does.

And it's made worse because we have a very heightened fear of mental illness in this country. I'm not an anthropologist or sociologist but you could probably talk to them and you would see a heightened societal fear of mental illness. If you're in the herd – yes? – and someone is acting in a way that is different to the rest of the herd – and I mean this is real amateur, shamateur stuff – I think we're probably conditioned to be nervous about people behaving perhaps slightly irrationally. I don't know why. But because we're sentient – is sentient the right word? – and clever we need to get over that. Because we have emotion, we have understanding, we have insight, we

need to get over that. There is no excuse. We don't want to
walk away from people with mental illness, we want to walk
towards them and embrace them, and we've really got to do
that. In the Bible, Jesus reaches out to people who we would
clearly now recognise as having mental health problems. So
we've got to be much more Good Samaritan about it.

Having OCD myself, I've probably developed levels of
empathy I wouldn't have otherwise had. I've been visited by
so many people in my constituency who desperately want
you to understand their mental health problems, because these
are really very serious problems. And before 'coming out' in
the debate I'd often, and it sounds cheesy, want to take their
hand, as I'm quite a tactile person, and say: 'Listen, I really
do understand.' Do you know what I mean? But now I can
be more honest, perhaps, in how I approach people, and give
them more of the reassurance that they're looking for. Because
I have an inadequate – in the sense that my own experience
is minor – but privileged insight into some of their fears and
concerns and what they are going through. So I can honestly
say that they're not out there alone.

Although I'm not perfect: there's a lot of people out there
who think I'm a total bastard and will continue to do so. Let's
be honest, I've had a lot of lovely letters from people saying:
'I'd never vote for you because you're a Tory, but thank you.'
And at the end of the day, I'm a member of parliament with
political views that many people won't like. So what I'm not
expecting is everyone to just say: 'What a lovely guy.' Like you
almost become like a pet, stroked on the head. Look, it's a part
of me. Sometimes people will say: 'What a decent guy', and
others will say: 'What a four-letter-man that Walker is.' Do
you see what I mean? It will not prevent me from doing things
politically that people don't like. You know, in politics you're
charged with making difficult decisions – such as putting 3p

on a litre of petrol – and you have to stand by those decisions. So it doesn't neuter you, it doesn't make you soppy, it just means that there's part of me, there are areas of my professional life, where I really think I have a good understanding of the problems and complexities faced by people.

Having said that, I've been on trains and someone very disturbed – someone probably with schizophrenia or who was psychotic – has been on the train and every instinct is to move away from them, it just is. I recognise this weakness in myself as well, I admit that freely, and actually you need to talk to yourself, you need to say: 'Sort yourself out Walker.' We've got to get over it, and it's a struggle, and we need to find ways to ensure that people who are very ill do get the support that they need, to either recover indefinitely or at least manage their illness and recognise the signs when it's coming on so they can seek help without being frightened. I think we need to address that by doing what parliament has now done, by what people in the media are doing: Alastair Campbell, Ruby Wax. Because by talking about it more we make it more everyday, more mainstream, and a lot of that fear will fall away. And that's what I was trying to do when I stood up in that debate and, judging by the feedback I've had, I've helped people – or *it* helped, what we did – and we're going to move the debate along.

★★★

So I'd like to say, if you're suffering from mental ill health: things are going to improve. I'm as confident as I can be that things are going to improve – that people are going to feel less frightened, less ashamed, in three to five years' time, than they do now, maybe even as early as next year. But things *are* going to change: the mood's changing, the media's changing, and parliament's now more comfortable with this. I have had letters from the Prime Minister and the leader of the opposition, both saying: 'This is where we need to be, this is good stuff, the debate was excellent.' So it's not going to happen overnight but it is beginning to happen, so that's a really good thing and that's something for people to hold on to.

I would also say to people suffering from mental health problems: you are certainly not alone, there is nothing to be ashamed of, and I and many others are thinking about you. We may not be able to reach all of you – we certainly can't reach all of you – but there are some really, really good strong people out there, both inside the NHS and outside the NHS, and in the voluntary sector, who want to make this a better place for you. We want to ensure that you can deal with your ill health earlier and sooner and get back to having a fulfilled, happy life, because being fulfilled in your life is a good thing. And the more people start to talk about these issues and become less frightened about them, the more people will get treated early and be back in the community doing the things they love to do: going out with their mates, having a job, socialising at work – all the fun stuff.

And I'd like to say to the public: you will all know someone – a relative, a friend, a colleague – who's suffering. So when you're sitting in your house, worrying about your child – feeling embarrassed and ashamed, not wanting the neighbours to know – just look across the street, look at your neighbours either side, and there's a fair chance there'll be another family behind that door having exactly the same fears and concerns you are. And wouldn't it be so much better and easier if we could all just talk about it together and then we'd all find that a problem shared is a problem spared and we could all get on and do something about it.

Do I have anything to add? Only that OCD has been part of me but it's never dominated me. There are times when, as I've said, it's been a pain, but it's a part of me as much as an arm is part of someone else, as much as arthritis is, and in a sense you just get on with it. I'm just delighted to be able to help. And I just want your – any – readers to know I'm not a saint: I'm short-tempered, I'm miserable, I'm grumpy and bolshy. But hey, do you know what? In twenty years' time, if my constituents keep me here and I'm still in parliament, or whatever happens, when I look in the mirror I'm not going to see a disappointed person looking back. I can't tell you how good that makes me feel telling you that. If I can look back in twenty years' time and I can say that standing up in that debate was the high point of my political career, then great, I had a high point. Does that make sense? I had a high point. I'm blissfully happy.

TASHA DANVERS

Former athlete and
Olympic medallist

'What would I say to the public about mental illness? Don't knock it 'til you've tried it! Do not knock it 'til you've tried it. Because, you know, it's easy to pass judgement but you never know what someone's going through . . . so just be a bit more understanding.'

Tasha Danvers was born in 1977 in London. A former elite athlete, Tasha represented Great Britain in the 1999 World Championships in Athletics, the 2000 Sydney Olympics, 2002 Commonwealth Games, and 2002 European Championships. In 2003 she married her coach, Darrell Smith, and took time out from her career to have a son, Jaden, in 2004. After making a return to athletics, the high points of her career included winning a silver medal at the Commonwealth Games in 2006 and a bronze medal in the 400-metre hurdles at the 2008 Beijing Olympics. After divorcing her husband in 2008 and struggling with injuries and depression, she attempted suicide, and later announced her retirement from professional sport just before the London 2012 Olympics. Since retiring, she has done some radio and television presenting and regularly gives motivational talks. The interview upon which this chapter is based took place in Bath, where Tasha lived at the time.

★★★

Depression paralyses you. That is definitely a major, major feature of depression for me: just paralysing. It's weird because you have all your faculties about you – you could do anything – but everything that you know you should do, or wanna do, just becomes impossible and people without depression do not understand it. There were so many days I would convince myself that I could do better the next day, that I *would* do better the next day, that I knew what it took to do better the next day. But the next day would come and you can't do it, so then you convince yourself again that tomorrow you'll be able to do it. But at the same time you're convincing yourself that you're going to do better, there's also that nagging voice that's reminding you that you failed at what you needed to do. And that feeds right back into the depression, so it's a vicious cycle.

It wasn't like there was one thing that started my depression. I think there were too many situations that I was not happy with happening at the same time. What's the word for that? Happening in conjunction. Looking back now, I think my depression started a lot earlier than I thought. I think I got depressed when I got married to my coach and was living in LA. I'd always had daddy issues and I knew I shouldn't have married who I married, but I did it anyway. I was so immature then. Like, you know, people say: 'You were twenty-six, you were grown.' But there's one thing being mature as a person and there's another category as being mature in relationships. And with men I was totally immature, I just basically said whatever they wanted to hear, but I really wasn't ready for that kind of commitment. So then mentally I was frustrated with myself for being in that situation. But I guess it's always easy to look back and say shoulda, coulda, woulda.

On top of that, financially it was just crap, and we were living with his parents. I was doing a lot of – most of – the contribution financially and I think, for a woman, that is a very frustrating place to be. I think you start to resent that person. And then you start to feel . . . it's just bad all round, and I think that's probably when it first started. Then I got pregnant, which I got ripped in the media for, cos it meant I had to miss the 2004 Olympics in Athens. And on top of that I had to watch my husband go to the Olympics, which was depressing. It was kind of difficult for me because my career sort of came to a halt and he was a coach so he still got to go out and enjoy doing what he was doing. So it was like a stream of unfortunate events.

Then my son Jaden was born and I'm an only child so I've never been around babies, while my husband was the eldest one of three. So he would come back and say: 'Oh why haven't you changed him and duh-duh-duh-duh', and, you know, I didn't want to change him . . . I didn't want to do anything. The first three months were a complete nightmare and I probably got more depressed then. Was it postnatal depression? I don't know what the definition is, but if the definition is: having a baby, then feeling depressed, then yeah, I felt that! I didn't feel like I was good enough and I didn't know what to do and I just . . . I did not enjoy it. When Jaden was born, people were like: 'Oh, you have this baby and you just have this rush of love.' I didn't have none of that. When my son was born it was just like: 'Oh, there's a baby.' It wasn't like: 'Oh, my heart just exploded', and all these fireworks that people go on about.

And then you feel even more crap about yourself because you don't feel anything. So I got down about not being a good mum and not having that so-called movie feeling that people always talk about, not feeling that I was living up to what my husband felt was right. You know: 'Why haven't you changed him, why haven't you done this or that?' 'I dunno, I don't want to, leave me alone.' The word depression didn't even occur to me at the time, I just knew I felt bad, I didn't like the situation. I didn't ever say: 'I'm depressed', it never really occurred to me to come to that conclusion. That's why, only after this more recent explosion of depression, going back I think: 'Um, I think I was probably depressed long before that.'

So I think having my son compounded the problems in the marriage and in 2007 I had just had enough. The relationship was at an all-time low and I had turned my attention else-where, I just didn't care anymore. So finally I said: 'Look, I don't love you.' But it was very difficult because during the phase where I realised I wanted a divorce it was in the build-up to the 2008 Olympics and obviously my husband's also my coach. So we've got to work together and then live together and, quite frankly, I don't like him. And he'd do bizarre things. I remember him knocking on my door at 3 o'clock in the morning before a race – not just a one-off little thing, we're at the World Championships – and saying: 'I want to talk about it', for hours and hours. But, you know, I was done already. Another time I remember one of the other coaches coming up to him during training, because he was acting strangely towards me and it was pretty obvious, and saying: 'Whatever's going on between you and Tasha, leave it outside.' This was at the Olympics, this was at the warm-up field of the Olympics.

But in training you learn to turn off. It's also how depressed people function. You have to get on with life so you put on your attire, your uniform, and you put on your face, and you do what you have to do to get through the day. And then you get back to your own space and you live in it – there's no other way to be. And sometimes you can do it well; sometimes not so well. In 2008 I'd come off a really good year professionally and I don't think I was as extremely depressed as I was coming up to London 2012, so it was just a bit easier to manage. I had a goal that I cared about and that was it. I'd missed out on 2004 because I'd had my son, so I was just really passionate about it. I worked my arse off to get to that point and the Games were brilliant. Other than the background noise – with my husband and all that – it was great; getting the bronze in the 400-metre hurdles was a fantastic feeling.

It was afterwards where it went downhill very fast, because I thought that if you put your full effort into something you get rewarded. I thought if I worked hard – and I'd given up a lot of other jobs so that I could solely focus on athletics – I could create a lifestyle for myself. So I thought: 'After the bronze things will change.' I knew that I wasn't going to become mega-rich – as track and field isn't often that kind of sport, especially for a 400-metre hurdler – but at least I'd be able to get a good contract. But I think the only offer I got was a $6,000 for the year contract. You might as well just spit in my face. I'd rather you just said no. Because when you see people being offered $60,000, $100,000, $250,000, and I'm offered six after I've got a bronze, that hurts. So I think I lost my enthusiasm at that point because I thought: 'What have I done this for?' You put all this effort in and you make all these sacrifices and then, at the end of it, someone's just like: 'Nah.' And that took away my motivation.

And then what happens is, when you're not in your right mind, your body follows, and I got injured a lot. The first year after '08 I did not want to run. I needed a break – I needed a physical and mental break because I'd been through a lot. I really did not want to run, I was just sick of it, but you have to: there are no days off in athletics, you have to just keep going. So I ran the Super 8 inter-city contest in Cardiff and I pulled my hamstring almost off the bone. Basically, the surgeon said if

I'd done any more I'd probably have had to have it sewn back on. So there was that and then the following year I popped my plantaris and I had to have surgery.

Then it all exploded through our divorce, which I filed for in December 2008, and when I came back to the UK in 2009 with Jaden that's when it all really went poorly. We were moving to Birmingham to live with a family member who had kids in the household and I thought it would be good for Jaden to be around them. Well, about two weeks or a month before we arrived everything went wrong, there was a major issue in the family, so instead of walking into the warm, welcoming environment that we had planned, we basically walked into a nightmare. So I've brought Jaden into this really depressed situation, and it was just rough. And I was travelling to London to train but I really had no help with Jaden like I thought I was going to have, as my family were unable to support me in the way we had intended.

So that was really difficult and then it just spiralled from there. My home situation: I wasn't happy with it. My financial situation: I wasn't happy with it. My life: I just wasn't happy with it! Everything about my life I just wasn't pleased with so it just goes from bad to worse. Long story short: Jaden left in January 2010 to go back to LA.

★★★

That year, after Jaden left, I moved to Bath and started training at the university there in preparation for London 2012. When I first moved I was very depressed, very all over the place, and no one here knew me so they didn't know that my behaviour was abnormal for me. So they just thought: 'Wow, she's different, she never wants to engage with the group, she warms up on her own, she doesn't really talk much.' Which is completely different to my normal personality, but they didn't know that. At my core, I am naturally bubbly, outgoing, friendly, I care about people, I'm silly, not embarrassed very easily. So depression is like an intrusion on who I am – as opposed to having changed who I am – if you know what I mean.

So when I'm not feeling good I interact the least amount possible. So, for instance, I'm not a very telephone-cally person anyway, I'm more email or text, but you definitely won't get me by phone when I'm depressed. When you're on the phone you have to keep up this conversation and I just can't be bothered. I don't want to answer no questions, I don't want anyone asking me how I am, or what's going on, I just don't want to put in the effort to try and engage in conversation. It's a lot of work. Whereas by text you can just say one thing and then get on with whatever you're doing – or get on with doing absolutely nothing, which is most likely what you're doing when you're depressed. So you just do enough to function if you can and some days were easier than others.

Training-wise I was just flat, everything was flat. And it was very difficult because in order to excel in sport you have to put in an extreme amount of effort. And when you don't even feel like getting up, putting that amount of effort into training is almost impossible. As an athlete other people expect so much of you, but there's also something unique about an athlete that makes them a good athlete and a successful athlete – it's in the way their mind works. We are very hard on ourselves as people. We don't often recognise how good we are, how successful we are, because the nature of what we do is always on to the next thing. So you have an achievement: 'Yeah, that was nice, now what can I do next?' You have such high expectations of yourself but it's impossible for someone to achieve that all the time, forever. Somewhere along the way it's going to take a drop and that's very hard for an athlete to deal with. Because, you know, having a goal and not achieving it says to an athlete: you're not good enough, you've failed. And nobody likes to feel like a failure.

But I just didn't have the fight or the motivation in me at the time, because when I'm depressed I just feel kind of, urh, lifeless, all day. There's a lethargic feeling, sort of no get up and go, no umph. Everything, you know, at this low-level drone. It's like a dark cloud that follows you everywhere. Some days it lightens up and then there's a few rays of sun but you just never know when it's gonna hit. It can really catch you off-guard because one minute you're fine and then the next minute you think: 'I couldn't care less', I'm just sort of a bit dead. And then I'll think: 'I'm alright again', and then suddenly I'll be watching something that wouldn't normally make me cry and I'll be bawling my eyes out. It's kind of like having your period – you're a bit more moody, or cranky, or more tearful or whatever – but it could come at any moment and last for God knows how long.

It wouldn't surprise me if there was a genetic thing going on because my aunt was admitted to a mental institute, my cousin committed suicide in 1998 at age twenty, a very close family member just admitted to me that he was suicidal recently, that he only stuck around because he wanted to see how I was going to do at the Olympics. Another person closely related to me went through a really bad stage where she was feeling suicidal and was totally depressed. And with what we know about the brain and how it's made up – physiologically, biologically, how it's actually structured – if there's a fault in a certain area it causes various behavioural patterns to be more prominent in that person. I mean, I'm no scientist but if your biology means that you inherit this flaw in your brain in the way it works then, yeah, it would not surprise me if there were some hereditary component.

So one day I was telling my sports doctor that I wasn't, you know, feeling up to . . . life. In order to have been able to do the things I needed to do, I literally would have had to have somebody living with me who would just take care of me. Somebody who would prepare everything, like all the food, as I couldn't even be bothered to eat junk food, let alone making high-quality meals. And I know this was quite hard for people who knew me to understand because I'm the one that everybody goes to for advice. I've always been that person; I'm always everybody's big sister. So normally I get the brush-off when I'm asking for help because everybody thinks that I'm going to be able to figure it out myself, because in their perception I'm so strong. But surely that means that when I *do* ask for help you would jump to it even more so, because you would think: 'Well, if she's asking for help then it must be serious.' But people would just say: 'Oh, you'll be alright, you know what to do.' Well, I may know what to do, but I just can't do it, so someone better just be on the lookout.

So I was just chatting to my sports doctor and he recommended taking these antidepressants. And I refused at first, but he kept bugging me about it, so I did take them from him but I never took them – if you see what I mean – I just took them so that he would think I was taking them. You know, when you read something on the box that says you could commit suicide because of taking them, you don't want to take this thing lightly. You hear a lot of stories about people who have. And no one's monitoring you, they just give you these pills and it's: 'Off you go, good luck!', which I don't really think is a good idea. And everyone else I talked to said: 'Oh, don't do that.' You know: 'Oh, my mother was a zombie when she did that, she was nothing like her normal self.' Or: 'These devastate your body', and blah, blah, blah. This was from friends

I knew who had known people on medication and also my mum, who didn't want me to because she's a natural health person, so she's studied a lot of these chemicals and is not a big fan.

But at that point, I couldn't do other things to help myself because I couldn't care less. For some people they might be able to trigger themselves to eat well or exercise, or there might be something that just allows them to snap themselves out of it, but I couldn't do it, not on my own. So although I think the natural way's the best way, there are times when you just can't, so after thinking about it for a long time, I eventually did end up taking the pills. I thought: 'Let's try it.' So I started taking one type and after a while I went to my GP and I said: 'These have helped me get a little bit better but it's kind of plateaued and I need to be a little bit more motivated to get out of bed.' You know, I had the motivation to put one leg out of bed, to not mind waking up, but I needed to be able to get out and do stuff, I wanted to do more. So I was put on another one and I was on that for about eight days. But during that time I'd spoken to my friend who was on antidepressants and she was like: 'Oh, you should try these ones because they actually give you energy, almost to the point where you have to tell yourself to relax a bit.' So I went back to my GP and I said: 'Well, my friend said to try these ones, what do you think?' And she was like: 'Yeah, sure.' So now I've had my normal ones, switched to the other ones, and about eight days later she let me have the new ones.

I felt a bit odd when I started taking them and they said: 'Oh that will just pass in time', but it wasn't just at first, this was ongoing. The problem was I didn't know what part was me and what part wasn't. I was still up and down emotionally and in training I'd feel dizzy and I would blink and feel like I was going to fall over. And every so often I'd get little injuries, or my training wasn't going well, or it would go well for a while and then it would plateau. And I'm like: 'What IS this? Is that me? Is it because I'm getting old? Or is it the drugs?' It was a nightmare. And because they were having such an effect on just my running, I'm thinking: 'Well, what else are they doing inside of me?' Because it's a chemical – do you know what I mean? These are very, very strong drugs, mind-altering drugs. And I didn't want to live like that, in some cloud of not knowing, so I knew I'd have to get out of that state eventually.

★★★

In the run-up to London 2012 we were training in South Africa in January and I think things had gone reasonably well there, but I knew that if we had any more problems injury-wise then it was gonna be a long shot. But to be honest by that point I'd lost my passion; it felt like something I had to do rather than something I wanted to do like in previous years. I wasn't doing it because I loved athletics or because I was passionate about it like in 2008. I cared because it was in London but that was the only reason I was doing it. But you can't tell anyone that stuff because you're supposed to want to be an Olympic champion. You can't say: 'I don't really want to do this, I'm just going through the motions.'

And in a way, you don't even want to admit to yourself that that's what you're thinking. You tell yourself that you *do* care every day when in actual fact you feel different. And then you feel stupid because this is the London Olympics, this could change your life if you get it right. So why would you not at least try? But it was arduous. I really didn't care, I just wanted to get it over and done with – the sooner the Olympics came and went the better. I should have retired before, you know: 'Done, boom, stick a fork in me', but because of London I kept going. But at that point it had become more other people's dream for me than mine. So that has its consequences and they don't fall on the people that encourage you to make the decisions, they fall back on you.

The day I took an overdose had been a good day. I'd had training, I'd started my session and it was going really well: I mean, like, I was on it. Then, just as we were about to get to the main part, I felt a weird pain in my leg so we called the session. And I was fine with that because the lead-up had been really good, so I wasn't bothered. Then I was driving home and I just started crying; I wasn't sad but I just started crying. That was infuriating to me and at that point I said: 'Well, if I can't even have a good day and not cry, and I don't even know why I'm crying, then this is ridiculous. I've tried and I can't do it and I've had enough.' So I drove home and I took all the sleeping pills that I'd been prescribed when I had insomnia. I was just like: 'God, I can't live like this. I can't live thinking I'm having a normal day and the next minute I'm crying. This is bizarre. I cannot function on a daily basis like this. I've had enough now, so goodbye . . . or hello!'

Then I texted my boyfriend, because I think a part of me wanted to let him know what I'd done, and I think as I was texting him I started to sort of fade out. I think he then, at that point, called my cousin who lives about 100 miles away from Bath and she called my mum before calling me. My mum said: 'Fine, I'm on my way up there already, just keep her on the phone, call the ambulance.' My cousin said it was really bad for her because I wasn't talking well and she could hear me falling over and knocking things over and I couldn't get to the door. And she's like: 'Oh my God, if I have to hear this it will haunt me for the rest of my life.' So she's just like trying to keep me on the phone.

Meanwhile, my mum was already on her way to Bath before

I'd even taken the pills, cos she'd been trying to get hold of me and I just hadn't got round to calling or texting her back. In her sixth-sense motherly way she knew there was something wrong before, but in my opinion there wasn't, because I was fine, I was actually fine, so I was surprised that she thought there was a reason to come up. And it's funny because she said: 'I knew there was something up', and I'm like: 'Mum, there really wasn't anything up.' Although I know it doesn't look like it, as when she gets there I'm in hospital!

So I woke up in hospital. I don't know what treatment they gave me, I just know I had all these pads on me. Then, when the psychiatrist was due to come round, my mum was like: 'There's a psychiatrist coming and they're probably going to want to section you.' And since I had an aunt who was admitted to the Maudesley Hospital in London and was so drugged up to her eyeballs that she didn't know her left from her right, I knew I didn't want people to section me and force me to take drugs. So I knew I needed to say what I needed to say, no matter what I felt, for everybody: for my son, for myself, for everybody. Because I knew that my mum could take care of me better than they could so I was not going to take the chance.

So I just totally blagged. I was just: 'I'm fine, it was just a bit of a mistake, blah, blah, blah.' I was: 'Yeah, it was a bad day.' I think I blamed it on the antidepressants, which I'm sure it was. I know it was connected to that because I wasn't that bad until then: all the emotional unpredictability was because of that. I'd had three different antidepressants in the space of a week and a half, and later, when I looked into it more, I found that you're not supposed to chop and change antidepressants just like that. Nah, not good, not good. So I just said: 'Yeah, I'm sure it was because of that and I'll be fine.' And I didn't have any more sleeping pills to not be fine with anyway, because I'd taken

them all! And they were more than happy to let me go home
and I was happy about that.

***

Because I didn't retire until a year later, there was no way I
could have come out at the time and said I was feeling suicidal,
or had attempted suicide. No way, not in public, absolutely
not, because you're showing weakness. It's not the reaction
of the public I'm concerned about but my competitors: why
would I want to give them that advantage? So you can't talk
about it. Sometimes you're all using the same doctor and are
on the same team, so can you trust them? It's a difficult beast
to tackle because there are so many reasons why an athlete
would not want to speak out while in the peak of their careers.
So where does that leave the athlete? Dealing with it on
their own.

So when I finally announced my retirement the following
year I was in heaven. Everyone was like: 'Oh, how are you
feeling? It must be really hard watching the Olympics.' Er,
negative! It has been great. A lot of depression comes from,
I think, when you're not living your truth: you're not where
you wanna be, doing a job you don't really wanna do, because
you feel you need to do it for the money. Or carrying on
doing athletics when you don't really want to because it's 2012
and who would quit before 2012? What sane person would
do that? So it's like . . . it just shows that when you are finally
living your truth, it's easier to move from day to day.

So when I was feeling good I called my GP and I said: 'How
do I wean off these antidepressants?' And she said: 'You don't,
you just get off them.' I think whatever it was, I was on the
lowest dose possible, but I thought she would say start splitting
them in half or something, but she said: 'Oh, just get off them

and if you have any problems give us a shout.' But I never had any problems. I feel proud of that because that was my goal: to not be on them. I never felt like it was a long-term option, because as long as you're putting chemicals inside your body, your body's not going to be in its natural, normal state that it's meant to be in. So to me, who wants to be as close to what I was born to be as possible, antidepressants are far from that. What with the side effects and differences in your personality, long-term there are too many downsides as far as I am concerned. They were just a crutch to get me to feel inspired to do the things I wanted to do, until I could take over and do them myself. It was about helping with the intrusion to the extent that I could help myself and I feel that I *am* helping myself now.

Now that I know that I have a propensity to be depressed it's a bit easier for me to stay aware, while before the situation could just take over my life without any action on my part. But now that I'm aware it's a condition – and it's a condition that I can do something about – I can more actively respond when I feel bad, because, at the end of the day, we all are in control of our own situation to a degree. And of course, the worse your depression is the harder it is to grab that control back – it's very, very difficult because, once you've fallen into that cycle, it is a very, very vicious cycle. So you feel crap, you don't do anything, and that causes you to create more situations in your life that make you feel crap. But you do have control ultimately; it's about getting back to where you have, and feel like you have, full control.

So it might be that I start telling myself: 'Well, what things do I, can I, appreciate?' Because depression is usually when you're feeling helpless and hopeless and out of control in your life, so you just focus on the areas of your life that you're not happy with. So I try to focus on what I *do* have – so gratitude basically. Okay, so I have a roof over my head at the moment, at least that's something. I've got a vehicle that I can get around with. I've got people that I know who, if I reach out to, will help me; you know, I've got good friends. So I try to switch my focus to positive things. I try to force myself to think about what's good about my life. The minute I start feeling down, what I've started doing is switching, trying to punch myself back, literally, and it's really, really difficult but I'm like: 'Come on Tash!'

Also, I try where I can – because I'm terrible with nutrition – to make sure that I'm putting good things in my body that will support my health, both physically and mentally, as there are certain things that we know are brain foods and help to lift your moods. I had a really great nutritionist back in America who told me that it is possible to pull yourself out of depression naturally but it takes three weeks minimum to see it turn around. If you're already depressed – or you're predisposed to depression – and you're not supporting yourself with nutrition then it's extremely difficult to get out of it, because you're feeding your mind with whatever you put inside. And chemicals, processed things, sugars and salts, are no good for your mind so they don't help you. Another thing: try to just get out and exercise, even if it's for five minutes. Loads of people hate doing exercise, even me. Oh yeah, I do *not* like exercise, I can't stand it, I really do not like exercising at all. I'm just lucky because it doesn't show. Do you know what I mean?

In addition to that I try to read things that I know will inspire me to take action. Books like *Lucky You* by David Hooper, *The Magic* by Rhonda Byrne, or *Amaze Yourself* by Jill Ammon-Wexler, about taking a quantum leap. The reason why I choose these books is that they empower you to take action, to take control of your own life. And although you may not act fully on everything you read, at least for that moment you feel inspired and in control of your own situation. So it's about just trying to armour yourself with things: having books around that are helpful, or positive-thinking CDs that you can fall asleep to that can change how your brain has been wired and shift some of the negative thoughts. I've used that kind of stuff a lot but I'm not a very routine person – I'll do it for a week and then not do it for three weeks – so it doesn't work for me for a long time. But for people who are routine it's great.

So the best thing for me – I can't speak for the world, that's for sure, because everyone's experience is different with depression, it's like a thumbprint – is when I am feeling good, to be extreme about the things that I know will work. So when I am feeling good I just go crazy about reading positive things, go crazy about eating well. Or, if I'm feeling positive, I might say: 'You know what, maybe I'll go and research places where I can go and talk to someone when I'm feeling depressed. I don't really need it right now but maybe on a day when I'm not feeling so motivated I'll have that information, so maybe I'll call.' Then if I do have a lapse, I have a bit more of a head start and maybe that lapse won't fall so deep. So always try to have a plan or something in the back of your mind because you never know when that might be able to click in and work for you.

And when I have done something positive, I really try to overly applaud myself for it. Because I *am* a person who is pre-disposed to being depressed, when I do actually do something it's a big deal. So, you know, I've been cleaning my house at the moment, getting ready to move, trying to get things boxed and packed on my own and the place looks like, I don't know, it's been derelict for three years and some squatter's been living there. But if a little space gets cleared, I say: 'You did well Tash, the bathroom's clean.' I'm like: 'Progress!' So I can feel proud. You know, if someone's feeling depressed and they took five minutes and went for a walk, or two minutes and went online and found out about depression, they need to really give themselves a proper 'well done' for doing it, because it's huge. I think that's really important. You might not have got to the big goal but you've got to recognise every single one of your tiny steps because there are no big steps without the little, tiny steps coming first.

Having said that, there are times when I also have to let myself be whatever I am, because the minute I start making judgements that's when it gets more difficult. Like: 'Oh, you should call these people, and you should talk to that person, and you should do some more work around the house.' So as well as applauding myself for what I have done, I make a point not to beat myself up for whatever I haven't done. You know, if the dishes have been there for two weeks and I sit there saying: 'You can't even clean up', I'll just drive myself deeper down into that feeling of lack of self-worth and being not good enough. And it doesn't serve the greater purpose of trying to stay positive, which is the opposite of being depressed, which is just very negative, very dark. So sometimes I'm just like: 'Okay, I'm feeling shit, I'll just sit here and feel shit for a while and just let it be and see how I feel tomorrow.'

So I guess the main thing is: 'It's okay: it's okay to be not okay. Sometimes you're not okay and that's okay.' The thing to be alert to is when it's going on too long – that's when I know I need to take some action. It's definitely majorly necessary to be alert to your moods all day and you've got to do whatever you've got to do to try to stop yourself from getting too far low, cos too far low means goodbye. But there is always opportunity, there is always a way to get out, it's just a matter of time and finding what's right for you and being patient with yourself. I think there is always light at the end of the tunnel. When you have a 'condition' – that's the word I like the most – that condition means I need to live my life differently and means I need to explore avenues of dealing with it. And, you know, it's still not perfect, I still get depressed, feel depressed, but it's easier to manage.

★★★

I've never faced any stigma personally but it must be there, because of the way people respond when they are, or think they are, depressed. I think the fact that people don't want to share it means that they must feel there's a reason why they need to hide it or be ashamed of it. And it does concern me thinking, in the future, about people being able to go online and find out that I've had this situation and whether it will affect whether they want to hire me, or wanna work with me, or whether they think I might just lose it at some point. So I haven't experienced that yet – and hopefully won't ever have to – but as we know how the world works, I think it's definitely possible.

So I think we need to be a bit more vocal about what depression is generally: making a big deal about it, but in a way that shows it's not the end of the world. Do you know what I mean? You know when you hear someone's depressed or suicidal you think: 'Oh, poor person.' You just get this image of this person who's all weak: a weak woman with her hair and clothes unkempt. But, you know, that's not always what depression really looks like: depression can look like a supermodel. So if people have a clearer idea of what it is, I think it will become less stigmatised, because people will begin to realise that it's way more common than they think.

I think it would be good for athletes to speak out more and to have more knowledge of what to do when they do speak out. I was fortunate because my federation did what it could to try and support me with my mental health issues. Other people aren't so lucky because their federations don't have any kind of support system. Who can they go to? Who can they talk to? Sometimes you can't even put into words how you're feeling so it's hard to tell anyone else. So people need help in what to say, how to get it out, how to tell people. So I think if more sports organisations and governing bodies had things in place and were welcoming if someone is willing to speak out, it would be good.

Because, whether we like it or not, athletes are looked up to, we're idolised, we're heroes, so what we say has an effect on people. Even when I spoke about it there was an athlete who contacted me and said she was really glad I'd come out because, even though she was only at club level, she had started self-harming because she wasn't achieving what she thought she should. And when she read my story she realised that she could just let it go. She said: 'Like, if you're an Olympic athlete and you can just say: "Enough is enough, I'm done", then I surely can so I've just moved on to other things now and I'm fine.' So even if, in speaking about my story, there was that one person on the planet who was able to make a different choice because of hearing it, then that's one less person. So if you can have a positive effect, then for me that was worth whatever negative may come from that.

So what would I say to the public about mental illness? Don't knock it 'til you've tried it! Do not knock it 'til you've tried it. Because, you know, it's easy to pass judgement. When I'm Twittering and I'm talking to people it's made me realise just how judgemental people are. But you never know what someone's going through, so I think people need to step back a bit, because it's easy to say you would do this and that when you're not in a situation, but you have no idea how you would respond when certain things are thrown at you in life. So I think people need to recognise that this is far more complicated than you think and it could be you one day. Because life might be going swell now but so many things cause people to be depressed – they might lose a loved one, lose a home – and major life changes can throw people into depression before they can bat an eyelid. So just be a bit more understanding. And if you do know someone who's depressed, don't assume you know how you can help them, just ask them: 'Is there any way I can help? Because if there is any way I can help then I will do my best.'

RICHARD MABEY

Writer, broadcaster, and naturalist

'I just ceased to be anything other than a person who is trapped in a toxic worry about their own worry. Bubbles like this occur: they are completely separate from what's outside. You are trapped in this self-referential cobweb of negativity.'

Born in 1941, Richard Mabey grew up in the Chilterns and was educated at the University of Oxford. He worked as a lecturer, and later as an editor at Penguin Books, before becoming a full-time writer in 1974. Since that time, Richard has written over thirty books, including: *Food for Free*, *Weeds: The Story of Outlaw Plants*, *Whistling in the Dark: In Pursuit of the Nightingale*, *Beechcombing: The Narratives of Trees*, *Turned Out Nice Again: On Living With the Weather*, and *Gilbert White*, which won the Whitbread Biography Award. He is also the author of the bestselling *Flora Britannica*, which won a National Book Award, and *Nature Cure*, his memoir, which was short-listed for the Whitbread, J.R. Ackerley and Ondaatje prizes. In addition, he has presented several television documentaries, is a regular contributor to BBC radio, and writes for the *Guardian*, *New Statesman*, and *Granta*. Richard has suffered from periods of anxiety and depression since he was a child, which culminated in a breakdown in 1999. He lives with his partner Polly Lavender in Norfolk, which is where the interview for this chapter took place.

***

I'm happy to talk about my environment when I was growing up but I would preface it by saying that I'm deeply disinclined to blame – if that is the word that one wants to use – anything that subsequently happened to me, or any part of my personality, or any defects in my personality, on anything that my parents did or didn't do to me. Being in the book business, one of the kinds of book that most repels me is the 'slag-my-parents-off' genre, which frequently turn out to be bestsellers. They seem to me often to indicate a refusal to take responsibility for yourself, which surely suggests that the authors are not yet recovered from whatever it is that is the matter with them.

But I guess there is a context. My parents were Londoners who, through the prescience of my father who saw the onset of war four years before a lot of other people did, moved my mother out to the Chilterns in 1936. I think it was a culture shock for both of them, moving into a quite conservative rural area. I'm not sure my mother was ever entirely happy with – no, happy's the wrong word, I'm not sure she was ever *comfortable* with – the edge-of-market-town kind of culture. She didn't make friends very easily so I think she was always a slightly lonely woman, although I would never have thought she was depressed at the time I knew her. She died twenty years ago now, before I had my serious illness, and in retrospect I suspect she probably *was* depressed.

My father seemed okay, not a greatly emotional man, but he was wrecked in his forties by having a premature heart attack and couldn't reconcile himself to the disappointments of a ruined career. He took to drink quite heavily, to the extent that he had more heart attacks, and then became a bed-bound alcoholic who ruled our household from his bed by the rather ruthless tactic of withholding money. So if we'd done things that appeared to be rather impertinent to him as a self-made man, like wanting to go to university, he wouldn't pay the electricity bill for a month. We'd live in the dark. And probably that made for a more troubled adolescence than it might otherwise have been. It meant, I suppose, that I had a greater responsibility as the man about the house when I was a teenager, which is not something you want on your shoulders at that age. And I think I was conscious of finding that irksome. Having subsequently been through a couple of years in which my own ambitions were totally (if temporarily) destroyed, and I started behaving in much the same way as him – retreating to my bed and drinking a lot – I now have a profound understanding of what he was going through. But at the time it was tough and I hated and resented my father for it.

However, one reason why I'm reluctant to put too much weight on that – even though it sounds like a classic dysfunctional family situation – is because I was showing symptoms typical of anxiety disorder from a very early age. My first things were gastrointestinal complaints at the age of about five. And I once had, when I was seven, hystericus globus – which is that sensation of a thing stuck in the throat – which enabled me to escape from the classroom and to run wildly about the town in a state of panic. In retrospect I can see that many of these devices, along with many psychosomatic exhibitions, are devices to get you back to a place of safety. And at that stage certainly I regarded home as being a much safer place than the outside world and school. So I got pretty skilled at hypochondriasis quite early on, although I don't think I had anything particularly original to say in the great drama of that art.

So maybe, if there was anything in that early period that triggered a tendency to retreat – to use the theatre of the body as a way of demanding attention from other people, and sometimes blame them at the same time: 'Look what you've done to me!' – I would say that it was not anything negative in those early years, but maybe a lack of anything positive. My parents weren't a demonstratively loving couple. I don't mean they didn't like each other, but they were not openly huggy and lovey, either to each other or to us. They weren't cold but there were no strong positive signals about the virtues of family life that radiated from the environment I grew up in. So if I'm to intellectualise what happened to me subsequently, it would be to do with a failure to be imprinted with the virtues of family life.

But really I'm disinclined to look for explanations. One ends up with a cocktail of influences going back generations, plus one's genetic makeup, through individual incidents, through atmospheres at particular moments in one's life. And one ends up who one is and I'm inclined to start with that rather than delve about looking for blame or seeking explanations, which one could never prove in any case.

★★★

I think the build-up to my breakdown in 1999 was a long, slow one. I suppose the first significant event was my mother's death. She'd had Parkinson's disease for twelve years and my younger sister and I had looked after her. We had professional help but basically she was ill at home and we stayed there, both of us, partly because of that. And, of course, as the confessions of many other anxiety sufferers and depressive hypochondriacs will tell you, there is nothing like the excuse of your own or somebody else's illness to keep you safe from more adult courses of life. So, retrospectively, I can see that as well as genuinely feeling it was a thing I should do as a moral duty – I loved my mother – I know that also there was a sub-agenda, that this gave me an infallible excuse for not having to go out and do that bit of growing up that I'd shunned or shied away from for so long.

So when she died that cut the ground out of that excuse, and at the time – that was 1993 – I was working on a very big book, *Flora Britannica*, which, in a way, occupied all my time and energy and commitment. And I can remember my very good, literate and insightful psychiatrist once saying: 'So you nursed the book instead', which I thought was a brilliant piece of insight. And I think that was true. But then the book was finished and I was in a curious position: living in a house which was mine by dint of being one of the family, with no big project on the stocks, feeling quite rocky. And knowing that my sister, contrary to me, feeling that now the maternal link was broken was all for getting on and starting her own life with her partner elsewhere. So I felt as if the kind of pegs I'd had in the ground – my sister and I looking after our mother, and the obsessive book work – were no longer there. And my troubles just started kind of insidiously at that point.

It began, I think, with generalised anxiety. Just a real uncomfortableness, waking in the morning. Sometimes you sleep well and then you wake up and you have a few seconds' peace, then it snaps in. I used to dread the mornings and that feeling. And the thing that happened, I suppose, was that it also began to be a self-generating process: that I began to be anxious about the anxiety that I knew was about to hit me. And so the whole thing began to be a vicious spiral that fed on itself until it was the only thing that I was thinking about. I was feeling anxious, and feeling anxious about feeling anxious, and feeling anxious about not knowing how the hell I was going to get out of it.

That then began to stop me doing things: I was reluctant to get out of bed because that started a cycle of new situations, which contained within them the potential for new actual anxieties, not just the intrinsic one. And I felt safer just being in that embryonic curl-up position in the bed for as long as I could. I used to go out at lunch and drink a great deal, go back, lie in the bed again. I stopped answering the post. I'd stopped being able to do any work at all, and I just ceased to be anything other than a person who is trapped in a toxic worry about their own worry. Bubbles like this occur: they are completely separate from what's outside. You are trapped in this self-referential cobweb of negativity.

At that point, drawing a line between anxiety and depression is, I think, one for the professionals. If you actually go through the scales of anxiety and depression, there ain't a great deal of difference between them. I suppose the thing that I didn't have that would have utterly, that would have comprehensively, put me in the depressive rather than the anxiety mode, was that I didn't have much problem with self-esteem. I didn't think I was a bad person. I felt a lost person, I didn't know why the hell this had happened to me and I wanted it to go away. But I didn't feel, for instance, that I was being punished for anything and I never really had any serious wishes to self-harm or take my own life.

Although I think one symptom that probably is depressive rather than anxious is to do with denying the good things that happened in your past, which is different from self-esteem. It is not being able to remember what it felt like to have done good things, to have done happy things, to have been an achiever. Lying in bed with a shelf of my own books looking at me, I was astonished, for instance, that I had ever been able to do that. It seemed inconceivable, with how I felt at that moment, that I once felt differently. You can remember the facts, you can remember that you did things, but you can't tag on to what it felt like. I couldn't click into how I could possibly have done them: what started them or what gave me the ideas. But regardless of what any specialist might label it as, certainly my internal experience was much more of a paralysing anxiety than of a depression.

So that's how it got to the stage where I went to seek professional help. I have to say I'm a lifelong believer in the welfare state, but the total lack of help I had from the national health system during my illness was just criminal, actually. I'm not blaming anyone, because I know the astonishing stress on their resources, but when I did go once I was given an appointment for an assessment *eighteen months* hence which, in fact, turned out to be much longer. I was patently in a bad state at this point and it must have been evident to the person who examined me that I was, and all he said was: 'We can offer you group therapy at some stage in the future but there is a long waiting list.' Then, after I had moved house and got better – three years down the line! – I actually got a letter through saying: 'We are now available to offer you an appointment for an assessment for group therapy.' I must have hit a very bad corner of a very stressed local system, but it was quite shocking.

So all the clinical help I got, I got privately, mainly with a doctor who was a straightforward talk-therapy man with CBT preferences. But although he was a fantastic man – extremely bright, we talked the same language – the sessions with him really didn't do much to help me and I think the reason I stayed with him was because I actually really liked him. He was an extraordinary guy with a great sense of humour, very well read, so we had agreeable sessions together, although they were not exactly cost-effective. I think people often go on with therapy for so long because it becomes terribly interesting to pry into one's past. But I think the statistical record for psychoanalysis, for instance, as a curative agent is very poor, and certainly the length of time that people are required to have it would suggest that it's not really a therapy at all. It's more a kind of intellectual . . . not game . . . but a support activity rather than a therapy, I think. When you engage in these dialogues about matters of the mind with another person who may or may not be interested in you, but is interested in hearing you talk, that is very flattering and it gives you something to look forward to. So theoretically – no, not theoretically, intellectually – I am now much more attracted by the theory of cognitive behaviour therapy, as it seems to me to wash away all that archaeology which can be seductively fascinating, but irrelevant.

I suppose maybe six months into that process – this must have been in about 2000 now – he recommended that I went as an inpatient to St Andrew's hospital in Northampton, where I was dried out and put on heavy duty drugs. I was on the maximum dose of – what was it at that point? – probably Paroxetine, I think, which is an SSRI. I was also on Heminevrin, Librium and Trazodone, which is halfway between an SSRI and a tricyclic, a sort of quadricyclic. And for the last few weeks of my second stay in St Andrew's I was given Risperidone, a major tranquilliser, although not for very long as it was quite zombie-making. But it really did calm me down more than anything else did. But in the end, although the drugs may have drawn a line in the sand and stopped me getting any worse and enabled me to actually get out of hospital, I was told by my doctors that I was then going to have to go to an institutional halfway house, rather than home, which I think they had correctly identified as being the pit in which I'd been immured and which, if I returned to, I would return to my old ways of thinking and probably drinking.

I think this was metaphorically also a piece of electric shock treatment, because I was totally horrified by this possibility, the weirdness of it and the absolute stripping away of the one place that had been my refuge and security. I've never had agoraphobia to the point of not being able to get out of the house but I had a long period when I was terrified of going abroad, that might even have started with my mother's illness. I mean it sounds a bit tidy, but I travelled on the continent when I was a student and had huge fun. But then there was a gap of maybe twenty years before I went again and it was a kind of ill-defined anxiety of not being safe when away from home. It absolutely dates back to running away from kindergarten with bouts of bad indigestion. And I suppose that is a kind of agoraphobia, it is an unwillingness to leave one's complete comfort zone, where you know you are in control, and that's an important thing for me. I'm not a control freak but I know I get most discomforted and confused when I am not in control of what I'm doing.

So they said: 'You're going to have to go to a halfway house.' But they did give me an alternative, which also makes me think that it was a slightly calculated threat. They said: 'If friends will look after you we will accept that.' I hadn't been sectioned but I had voluntarily given some of my friends power of attorney over me at the point when I was not paying bills and things like that. So there was no way that I could, legally, do a runner. I had to take one of those two options because, in the strict letter of the law, decisions of that sort now rested with my attorneys not with me. So that was the deal that was worked out: that I would not go fleeing back to the Chilterns – and crawl back to my bed, with cycles repeating themselves – but that I would go to friends.

And, bless their hearts, a succession of them worked out this rota for me, most of it in north Norfolk, which they turned into a kind of boot camp on the way. The first two friends that I stayed with for some weeks on the Norfolk coast really put me to work. I'd put on a lot of weight, so I was fed properly, and I was expected – and this is why I call it boot camp – to do more than my fair share of housework: washing and washing up, tending the vegetables. And I found it really hard work to start with because I'd been so inactive; I was physically in a very run-down state as well. People who've never been depressed don't understand that depression is a physical illness as well as a mental one. I was very weak, my muscles were very weak, and I found all these things quite a labour. And when I was taken out for my daily walk – on a lead almost – I was completely gutted after about a quarter of a mile. But, week on week, all these things started to improve. And as I toured round various friends, miraculously, or mysteriously, or maybe very obviously under that sort of normal, rather strict – but very affectionate – attention, I began to get better, very, very slowly. My senses began to come alive again.

★★★

When I was seriously ill, what I found didn't happen to me was the idea – that's now rather fashionable as a therapeutic notion – that if you simply get people out into the countryside or amongst greenery then it helps make them better. And the statistics are impressive, including ones that are really quite extraordinary. Like if you put a landscape painting on the ward wall of people who've had surgery, their wounds heal faster than if there isn't one. It seems extraordinary but the experiment's been done and peer reviewed. That didn't happen with me. Exactly the opposite happened, in that I found it completely counterproductive to try to go out into the natural world, because the one bit of my feeling that I did remember

– even if a lot had gone a bit blank – was that out there had really turned me on. To take walks and see things and to feel completely unmoved by them was shocking to me, so I stayed away from that. I know it does work with other people, perhaps at a slightly lower level of illness than I had, so I'm not damning that, I'm just saying that didn't work for me.

It may be going off too far sideways for me to say what I think about this trend of nature therapy, which I wholly approve of, but only if it is done with great honesty. I think that the idea that nature makes you happy – big capital N, capital H – is ridiculous, insulting to nature, belittling of you. We can sit here today – fabulous day, everything looks good – and I know for a fact there's catastrophe out there at the moment. That this extraordinary weather system has killed millions of migrating swallows and other birds. It seems to me that nature can be an enormous enhancer of emotional intelligence, if you get people to grasp the whole truth about it. Because then it becomes a play in a way. It's something happening with which you are connected, but you can also view it slightly objectively. And the truth is that there are a hell of a lot of bad things that are happening out there – some of which are our fault and some of which are inherent to being alive – but that life comes through. And that was the 'nature cure' that was in there: sometimes simply glimpsing, at closer quarters than I ever had before, the ingenuity of life in surviving.

I think, having been to a dark place myself, I saw the dark things that were happening in nature more closely, more sympathetically. But that also opened me up – as this changeable East Anglian landscape did itself – to seeing the ways in which it would not give in. That wonderful line that Jeff Goldblum says in *Jurassic Park* when the dinosaurs manage to live, despite attempts to stop them breeding: 'Life will find a way.' And I thought: 'Yeah, life does find a way.' And that was something

that I grasped very soon up here, and it was a powerful therapeutic thing for me. And it was not just a personal revelation,
but changed my professional life as well, because it hardened a
theme in my writing, that I'd always just played with before,
that we treat nature too much as a pet. We want to be mother
and father, we believe it can't possibly survive without our
intensive care, whereas in fact it's much tougher, more resilient,
more ingenious, more devious than that. I now see, and am
moved by, and can argue the case for, how things get through,
and to celebrate that 'poetry of survival', as John Fowles once
called it.

I take risks now, at least within my own sphere of confidence, that I never would have before. And I'm a much bolder
person, I'm much friendlier, I was always timid of strangers
and unfamiliar situations before but I'm just the opposite
now. Getting better hugely built my strength and confidence
– not just restored them, because they were probably a bit
shaky before – but actually built a whole new steeliness inside
myself which had not been there before. And, as I said, that
spread into a much more thought-through philosophy about
how I would write about my subject, in which that was
reflected.

So I think I would say to other sufferers that one person got
through: I did. Anybody can; almost anybody. People do get
better. But I don't think you can ever get better just by other
people making you better. I think at some point there has to
be that personal moment of revelation, which I had moving up
here when I saw somehow that the world was more resilient
than I thought and I was lifted by that. And that was the nucleus
of getting well. If you can reach that with other people's help
that's fine but I think there is a point where you do have to
make a commitment yourself. You can't simply rely on things
like having drugs: you have to want to, you have to make that

decision yourself. So I would say you can get better but you need to want to at some point.

★★★

I'm off-message about depression because I think we regard it too negatively, if it's possible to say that. The automatic assumption that it is an appalling thing to happen to someone – all the dark imagery and the way people talk about 'fighting depression' – that it would be better if it didn't happen, that it comes in some way from beyond oneself. I got very interested as I was recovering and writing my memoir *Nature Cure*, in the occurrence of depression in the natural world. What one would call depressive forms. Because whatever its complexities, and whatever its specific causes, depression manifests itself in human beings inside a form which is widespread in the natural world in many living things. The idea that – let's just stick with humans for the moment – that we react to trouble, to strife, to stress, with the two things we always talk about – flight or fight – is a huge simplification. Throughout the evolution of life there's been a third way between those two, which is retreat. If fight or flight prove impossible, difficult, incomprehensible, then you retreat into yourself. Playing possum is one. Large numbers of creatures go into conditions of protective unconsciousness when they're endangered. Their nervous systems, if one was to measure their activity, would very closely resemble those of human depressives: the parasympathetic takes over.

Oliver Sacks is one of the few neurologists who's written about this wonderfully, in his book on migraines, which he classes as one of those forms of what an earlier psychologist called 'vegetative retreat'. That is: if you can't beat them, curl up in a ball and wait 'till it's gone away. Now this works if you're a hedgehog and the badger does go away. But when the badger is perhaps metaphorical and doesn't go away then that's when we're in trouble. But I do think that that lesson, that one's nervous system is not behaving in some unearthly way when these weird things happen to you, but it is an entirely natural response, is useful. It's a response to a situation that is intolerable but for which you can think of no easy way out – like fighting or flighting – and so you just stick.

So to begin with that and to say: okay, when you've gone into this state you've actually done something rather sensible and what you need to do now is to listen to that and see that it is a signal. That there is some particle of your life, or existence, or environment, that you need to get away from or change. Just as it would be if you were an animal that had gone into temporary shock, waiting for . . . again, showing psychosomatic symptoms . . . I hadn't thought of that before, it's a piece of theatre for the other creatures watching it. And what the process of therapy, or adaptation, then becomes is understanding what it was that, at that moment, caused you to believe that you were unable to do anything about it.

I had some weird, sensory strangenesses during my illness. Auditory hallucinations – no, not hallucinations because I knew they were not real – just auditory phenomena, which, for some reason, my ears had conjured up. And it was quite odd because each ear had its own particular thing. A bass, who could have come from the Russian Orthodox Church, was singing very deeply in one ear and a sort of country band playing light music was playing in the other. Fortunately, they very rarely both did it together! It was an amusing thing, in retrospect. I quite quickly – I wouldn't go so far as to say saw the funny side of it all – but got to realise that what these anxiety/depression periods are doing to you, is a kind of comedy. It is a disruption of the normal order of your life, which I think is intended for you to – as a really good comedy by Shakespeare would – rethink some of the things that are going on.

Subsequent to having vaguely written something along these lines in *Nature Cure*, I met a Buddhist psychotherapist. I have no particular feelings about Buddhism one way or another: I think it has a lot of very good points about acceptance, but I don't like its nihilism and lack of affection for the physical world. But its attitude to depression, I found, is pretty much that you accept the illness as something entirely natural that's happened to you because you've got, or have been put, in a position where you can see no other way out. So the therapy is to, as it were, embrace the depression, not try to fight it, and to work out what the way out is. Which, I suppose, is what all the therapies are, but it just starts from that different position of not regarding the depression as an enemy but as a potential teacher. And I think I've come to regard my illness as that: that having recovered from it I learnt an enormous amount about myself.

I don't think that I really grasped the notion of taking full responsibility for my emotional life until I'd been ill. I think that being ill was the climax of a long build-up of a failure to take responsibility, which in the end forced me to make that decision to take responsibility. So it had a function, it wasn't a random demonic bolt from the blue. And those failures to take responsibility are linked to that failure to have picked up a positive image of family life, evidenced by the fact of my remaining single for most of my life. I had enormous numbers of relationships but ran away from all of them. I was a classic commitment phobic. And probably really rather nasty in that I think I was quite an attractive guy – I had a number of very glamorous girlfriends – and I entered into relationships with an initial willingness, which in any honest other person would have raised the expectations that things would go further. But

as soon as the possibility of a commitment, of living with somebody arose, I panicked and ran away.

I suppose the nest that I'd built for myself in the family home
was one place I did feel secure, even though that sounds to con-
tradict what I've said about family security. I was still tied to
my home, not so much to my mother's apron strings – because
she was getting ill in this process – but I had some secure emotional roots in, as it were, another person's existence, or another
group of people's existence, which was my family's home, rather
than something which I'd built myself. And a failure to actually generate it for myself, if I am to be tempted into giving an
explanation, was because I'd failed to absorb evidence of it being
a viable course for me. So I do not regret one second of having
been ill because it made me change my life. It made me get out
of that enveloped home in which I was locked – which was kind
of unconsciousness in itself – and get out and build a life of my
own. To fledge, as I put it at the beginning of *Nature Cure*.

Nature Cure is not a self-help book, it's a memoir, it's what
happened to me. But I do think that the worst possible way
of starting one's journey back is with the assumption that you
are dealing with something diabolic. I don't mean that literally
– diabolic: to do with the devil – but that illness is a merciless
enemy that has to be fought off, rather than reflected on. If
instead one could say: okay, this is happening, it's a part of my
life, let's begin by being calm about it. A Buddhist would say
thank you for depression. Because it may be about to, as it did
for me, prise open something that is wrong with your life and
turn it into something new. If you're lucky; you have to be
lucky for that. I know very well that it often goes the opposite
way. But it seems to me that's not a bad way to start. Of course,
everybody has to work out their own solution, with the people
close to them and with their clinicians. But that would be my
philosophy to underpin any therapeutic approach.

So that leaves me in the position of . . . what? Of not wishing depression on anyone as kind of an essential part of your education – you know, you can't be a proper human being unless you've had a good session of it – but at least saying that if it does happen to you, don't regard it as the enemy. Don't regard the experience as necessarily being one of unmitigated disaster, but perhaps begin the long journey back by saying: okay, this has happened to me for a reason which may actually be of help to me as a human being in the end, rather than just wiping out several years of my life. And that's easier said from a position of having got better, I know, I say that with absolute humility. But for me that's been true.

The thing that shocked me – that really deeply disappointed me – was when people said to me: 'You're so brave to admit all this in *Nature Cure*.' It had never crossed my mind that it had anything to do with bravery. Maybe that's the result of being a writer: that it's in the nature of things to want to explore them and discuss them publicly, so maybe I'm a special case. But I truthfully had never thought what other people obviously had thought: that there would be consequences of confessing this in public. There weren't. On the contrary, it was just the opposite, and the idea of the stigma against mental illness – which I know full well exists – is mysterious to me because it's not something I've ever experienced.

I shall always be a little shaky emotionally but the bad days – the bad weeks sometimes – that I have, are never too serious. I always bounce back. I know that it is in my nature to express things that are going wrong in my life physically in some ways. Nothing particularly seriously – I get the full run of chronic ailments that most of us get – but, and again I hope this is consistent, I tend to regard those as: this is me, this is how I work, it's not an illness. I mean, much of the time I wish it wasn't there, but I tend to say: 'Okay, it's a bit like having one leg longer than the other, it's a nuisance but it's who I am.' So that's, again, a slightly Buddhist reconciliation with the facts of one's frailty, that instead of constantly saying: 'Oh my God, I wish I felt better' to say: 'I've got a bit of a morning headache, I'm feeling a bit worried today, okay, get on with it, or get over it. It's not the end of the world. It's just the continuity of you.'

Afterword

By Dr Richard Bowskill

Reading this collection of powerful and moving personal accounts of well-known individuals' experiences of mental distress reminds me that being a psychiatrist is a humbling and unique profession. During my day at the office, I have the privilege of treating the whole spectrum of society: from the homeless to the aristocracy, 'ordinary' people to 'celebrities'. Yet despite the differences in people's circumstances, I regularly hear strikingly similar accounts of the complex and distressing symptoms of mental illness. For mental illness – or the more self-contradictory term of 'mental health condition' – is a great equaliser; it respects no boundaries of age, race, culture, wealth, or intellect. Thus, while the accounts in this book may be the experiences of unique people, their stories are common to many.

These testimonies are a valuable contribution to the literature. They give a rich insight into the confusing world of a variety of mental health problems and have the potential to help others manage their distress. Mental illness is part of the human condition and sufferers usually experience a vast and frustrating array of emotions and thoughts. One of the most distressing aspects of mental illness can be the feeling that you are alone with your suffering: that no one understands, that you are the only one to have gone through such discomforting experiences, and the fear that you are descending into madness. Hearing that famous, capable individuals can experience these mental conditions can be a great comfort and ease the burden of solitary suffering.

I also believe that this book will encourage those suffering from mental illness to reach out for support, access and accept treatment, and begin their recovery journeys. There is a myriad of therapies, medications, and self-help techniques available out there and it can be a daunting task to choose between them. So how do people decide how and why to seek help, and what that help might be? In recent research that my colleagues and I conducted on bipolar disorder it rapidly became apparent that individuals do not appraise scientific literature in order to decide whether to take Lithium, or an SSRI, or to undergo art therapy. Instead, decisions about treatment are strongly influenced by anecdote, hearsay, and other people's accounts of what worked for them. So I believe that these stories – which bring to life celebrities' personal struggles with a range of common mental illnesses, what treatments they have tried, and their successes and frustrations – will be very powerful tools in motivating others to seek treatment, because: 'If it works for them, it can work for me.'

These accounts are also helpful on a societal level. For despite the prevalence of mental illness – and the recent advances in understanding and treatment – there remains a widespread social stigma attached to it, born mostly out of ignorance. The mentally ill may no longer be tortured, lobotomised, sterilised, or executed, as in past centuries, but according to a recent survey nearly nine out of ten sufferers still experience negative reactions to their conditions. In extreme cases this is described as worse than the illness itself, discouraging openness, making people feel ashamed, and isolating sufferers. I therefore hope that these stories can help to raise general awareness and knowledge about mental health and dispel some of the more persistent and damaging myths and stereotypes surrounding it.

So what does this book ultimately leave us with? As a practising psychiatrist it reinforces to me how mental illness can affect *anyone* and, at times, be a source of enormous distress. However, as it further illustrates, those who live with mental illness may still be among the most successful people in their professional fields and lead happy personal lives. Mental disorder is not necessarily a bar to having a fulfilled life. Rather, it is something that can be lived with, treated, recovered and learned from, and in this sense these stories are positive ones of hope and triumph over adversity.

Dr Richard Bowskill, MA MRCP MRCPsych
Consultant Psychiatrist and Medical Director

Factsheets

Depression

What is depression?

Everyone sometimes feels a bit down or blue, but being clinically depressed is something very different. Depression, which is a type of mood (or affective) disorder, may be diagnosed when a person suffers from a low mood that lasts all day every day over a prolonged period of time, or comes and goes repeatedly, adversely interfering with their life.

What are the symptoms of depression?

People suffering from depression may have emotional, behavioural, physical, and cognitive symptoms. These may include feeling sad, having negative and pessimistic thoughts, taking less pleasure in activities that are usually enjoyable, and feelings of low self-esteem and self-confidence. People who are depressed may also have less energy than normal, feel tired all the time, find it hard to concentrate, and suffer from memory problems. They may feel guilty, worthless, numb, in despair, irritable, impatient, restless, anxious, and/or agitated. They may also eat and sleep less or more than normal, cry a lot, lose their sex drive, and have unexplainable physical symptoms. In the most serious cases, sufferers may also have suicidal thoughts and may attempt, or commit, suicide.

Are there different types of depression?

MILD DEPRESSION: People suffering from mild depression usually feel in generally low spirits and have two or three of the symptoms listed above but can continue with most of their day-to-day activities, although these may be more of an effort.

MODERATE DEPRESSION: People suffering from moderate depression frequently have extreme difficulty continuing with their daily lives, and have four or more of the above symptoms.

SEVERE DEPRESSION: People suffering from severe depression have many of the above symptoms, including suicidal thoughts and attempts, and may need to be treated in hospital.

POSTNATAL DEPRESSION (PND): It is thought that up to 85 per cent of women experience a low mood after giving birth, commonly called the 'baby blues', which usually gets better by itself. However, around 10–15 per cent of new mothers develop PND, which is a more serious and longer-lasting condition. As well as suffering from the usual symptoms of depression, women suffering from PND may also feel unconnected to, or hostile towards, their baby and/or partner. PND may be caused by hormonal changes, a lack of support, major lifestyle changes due to having a baby, social circumstances (such as poor living conditions), and previous mental illness.

How common is depression?

It is thought that around 10 per cent of the general population is suffering from depression at any given time.

Are certain types of people more likely to develop depression?

Anyone can become depressed, including children, adults, the elderly, men, and women. However, it has been found to be more common in females, people of a lower socio-economic status, and those who are unmarried.

Why do people get depression?

Depression is usually the result of a combination of factors:

GENES: Some forms of depression, such as bipolar disorder (see bipolar disorder factsheet), seem to be highly influenced by genes. More common forms of depression have less clear genetic roots, although depression may often appear to run in families.

ENVIRONMENT AND LIFE EXPERIENCES: Distressing events or circumstances as a child (such as poor parenting, sexual and physical abuse) and/or as an adult (such as divorce, bereavement, and work stress) may trigger episodes of depression or make a person more likely to develop it at a later stage.

BODY CHEMISTRY: Abnormal levels of neurotransmitters in the brain (such as lower serotonin levels) and hormonal changes (such as those that occur in pregnancy and menopause) may also trigger depression.

PHYSICAL ILLNESSES: Illnesses (such as an underactive thyroid) can cause depression, and some medications (such as beta-blockers) may also have depressive side effects.

What is the treatment for depression?

Most cases of depression can be treated at home, although hospitalisation may be needed for severe cases, particularly if a person feels suicidal.

LIFESTYLE CHANGES AND SELF-HELP MEASURES: In milder forms of depression, healthy eating, exercise (such as walking, swimming, or yoga), good sleep hygiene (such as getting up at the same time every morning and not napping in the daytime), and avoiding drugs and alcohol may help alleviate symptoms. Self-help materials – which may include information on mood monitoring and management of symptoms – and self-help groups (face-to-face or online) may also be beneficial.

ALTERNATIVE AND COMPLEMENTARY THERAPIES: Some people also find treatments such as homeopathy, aromatherapy, massage, and acupuncture helpful. In addition, some studies have found the herb *Hypericum perforatum* – commonly known as St John's Wort – to be as effective as antidepressants in relieving mild depression. (This should not be taken alongside standard antidepressants.)

TALKING THERAPIES: In moderate to severe depression, talking therapies – which may include psychotherapy, interpersonal therapy (IPT), counselling, and cognitive behavioural therapy (CBT) – are usually recommended. CBT is currently the most commonly used talking therapy and broadly involves identifying negative thoughts, feelings, and behaviour and trying to replace these with positive ones.

MEDICATION: Antidepressants, usually in the form of selective serotonin reuptake inhibitors (SSRIs), may also be prescribed. If these don't work, tricyclic antidepressants or monoamine oxidase inhibitors (MAOIs) may be tried.

ELECTROCONVULSIVE THERAPY: ECT may still occasionally be used for severely depressed people who have not responded to other forms of treatment.

What are the risks associated with depression?

Depression may make people more likely to suffer from physical health problems, such as diabetes, cardiovascular disease, and strokes. Over half of people who suffer from depression also have an anxiety disorder, and some may self-medicate with alcohol and drugs. Those with severe depression are at increased risk of self-harm, suicidal feelings, and committing suicide.

What is the prognosis for people with depression?

Many people with depression, particularly in its milder form, go on to make full recoveries. However, around half of people who have one episode of depression will have at least one more during their lifetimes, and for about one person in five the condition becomes chronic. The earlier that people get the right treatment, the better the outcome.

Who can I contact for help if I think I have depression?

Your first point of contact should be your GP, who will rule out any physical or medical problems that may be causing your depression. Depending on the severity of your symptoms, they may then refer you for talking therapy (usually CBT) and/or prescribe antidepressant medication. If you have severe depression and may be at risk of harming yourself, have psychotic symptoms, or do not respond to standard treatments, you may be referred to your local community mental health team (CMHT). In addition, the below organisations may be able to offer help, support, and advice:

Depression Alliance
Tel: 0845 123 23 20
Web: www.depressionalliance.org

Depression UK
Email: info@depressionuk.org
Web: www.depressionuk.org

Mood Swings Network
Tel: 0161 832 3736
Web: www.moodswings.org.uk

Black Dog Tribe
Web: www.blackdogtribe.com

Pre- and Postnatal Depression Advice and Support (PANDAS)
Help Line: 0843 289 8401
Web: www.pandasfoundation.org.uk

Please see the 'Useful contacts and links' pages for more resources and organisations that may be able to help, including national mental health charities such as Mind, Sane, and Rethink.

Bipolar disorder

What is bipolar disorder?

Formerly called manic depression, bipolar disorder is a severe mood (or affective) disorder. The condition is characterised by extreme mood swings, from episodes of overactive, excited behaviour, known as mania, to deep depression. Between the 'highs' and 'lows' there can be periods of stability and normal mood.

What are the symptoms of bipolar disorder?

MANIC EPISODES: During manic episodes people with bipolar disorder typically feel euphoric, high, and elated, or restless and irritable. They may talk very fast, have racing thoughts, be unable to concentrate, and need little sleep. Sufferers often have an inflated sense of self-importance and poor judgement, and may exhibit risk-taking behaviours such as excessive spending, sexual activity, drug and alcohol use, and/or aggressive behaviour. Some people may also be highly productive, driven, and creative.

DEPRESSIVE EPISODES: Conversely, symptoms during depressive episodes may include a sense of hopelessness and worthlessness, feelings of emotional emptiness, and guilt. During such lows, sufferers may experience chronic fatigue, sleep too little or too much, lose or gain weight, lose interest in daily life, and take no pleasure in normal activities. They may also have recurrent thoughts about death or suicidal feelings, and some may attempt suicide. Around half of people with severe bipolar disorder also have psychotic symptoms, including hallucinations, and/or delusions.

Are there different types of bipolar disorder?

BIPOLAR I DISORDER: BP I is defined by manic episodes that last at least a week, or by severe manic symptoms that need hospital treatment. Usually, but not always, the sufferer also has depressive episodes, which last at least two weeks.

BIPOLAR II DISORDER: BP II is defined by a pattern of depressive periods interspersed with 'hypomanic' episodes, which involve mild or moderate (rather than full-blown) mania. Some people describe this hypomania as pleasant and it can be associated with productivity and creativity.

CYCLOTHYMIC DISORDER: People suffering from cyclothymia have recurrent episodes of hypomania and mild depression for at least two years. Although considered a less severe form of bipolar disorder, cyclothymia may still affect people's daily functioning.

RAPID-CYCLING BIPOLAR DISORDER: Those with rapid cycling experience four or more episodes of major depression, mania, hypomania, or mixed symptoms within a year. Some people may have more than one episode in a week, or even a day.

BIPOLAR DISORDER NOT OTHERWISE SPECIFIED: BP-NOS is diagnosed when a person has symptoms of the illness (which are outside their normal behaviour) that do not meet the criteria for either bipolar I or II.

How common is bipolar disorder?

It is thought that 1–2 per cent of the general population suffer from bipolar disorder, although up to 4–5 per cent may be on the bipolar spectrum.

Are certain types of people more likely to develop bipolar disorder?

Women may be slightly more likely to be affected by bipolar disorder than men. The condition usually develops in the late teens or early adulthood, with around half of all cases starting before the age of 25. However, the disorder is commonly not correctly diagnosed for around ten years, with an average of 3.5 misdiagnoses before this.

Why do people get bipolar disorder?

There are thought to be several factors involved in the development of bipolar disorder:

GENES: Although no one particular gene is responsible for causing bipolar disorder, it does seem to run in families, with close relatives of people with the condition being at greater risk of developing bipolar disorder than other people.

ENVIRONMENT AND LIFE EXPERIENCES: Factors such as childhood abuse and trauma, bereavement, relationship or work stress may also act as triggers in a person already predisposed to developing bipolar disorder, or bring on episodes in an existing disorder.

BODY CHEMISTRY: People who have bipolar disorder often have higher levels of the stress hormone cortisol than other people, while those in manic states have higher levels of the neurotransmitters norepinephrine and dopamine. Abnormal thyroid hormones and elevated insulin levels have also been linked to bipolar disorder.

What is the treatment for bipolar disorder?

The aim of treatment is to reduce the frequency and severity of symptoms. Most people can be treated at home but, in severe cases, hospitalisation may be needed.

MEDICATION: Mood stabilising drugs are the primary treatment for bipolar disorder and are usually taken on an ongoing basis. Lithium, which has been used for over sixty years, is the most commonly prescribed medication, but anticonvulsants, antipsychotics, antidepressants, and benzodiazepines ('tranquillisers') may also be used.

TALKING THERAPY: Talking therapy may also be helpful, with cognitive behavioural therapy (CBT) being recommended for the depressive states and also to help people recognise symptoms early on and so prevent relapse. Family therapy may help sufferers and their relatives to deal with the distress that the disorder can cause.

SELF-EDUCATION, SELF-HELP MEASURES, AND SELF-MANAGEMENT: Such treatments may include mood monitoring, coping skills, exercise, nutrition, regular sleeping patterns, and avoiding stress, as well as learning about the illness, its treatment, and signs of relapse.

What are the risks associated with bipolar disorder?

Bipolar disorder may be associated with other mental health problems, self-harm, alcohol and drug abuse. Some studies have found that people suffering from bipolar disorder have a 15–20 times greater risk of suicide than the general population.

What is the prognosis for people with bipolar disorder?

On average, people with bipolar disorder have five or six episodes over the course of twenty years. However, with early diagnosis and proper treatment, people are often able to significantly stabilise their moods, improve their symptoms, and live relatively normal lives, despite the recurrent nature of the illness.

Who can I contact for help if I think I have bipolar disorder?

Your first point of contact should be your GP, who may refer you to a psychiatrist on the NHS for assessment and treatment. They may also put you in touch with a community mental health team (CMHT), early intervention service (EIS), crisis service, and/or assertive outreach team, who can help with assessment and treatment, usually in the home. There are also day hospitals that can be visited every day or as needed. In addition, the below organisations may be able to offer help, support, and advice:

Bipolar UK
Tel: 020 7931 6480
Email: info@bipolaruk.org.uk
Web: www.bipolaruk.org.uk

Equilibrium – The Bipolar Foundation
Web: www.bipolar-foundation.org

Please see the 'Useful contacts and links' pages for more resources and organisations which may be able to help, including national mental health charities such as Mind, Sane, and Rethink.

Anxiety disorders

What is anxiety?

Everybody feels anxious sometimes and it is usually a perfectly normal and, indeed, helpful response. For example, some anxiety can enhance energy and performance when doing exams, in job interviews, or speaking in public. People also experience anxiety in situations where there is a threat, such as being attacked by an animal or person. This anxiety triggers the body's natural 'fight or flight' response – where adrenaline is released into the bloodstream, triggering physical changes such as an increased heart rate and breathing – which helps the person to put up a fight or run away. The anxiety then naturally subsides once the situation is resolved. However, anxiety can become a problem if a person feels excessively anxious on a regular basis for no obvious reason, or in relation to situations, objects, or events that do not cause most other people anxiety. In extreme cases, anxiety symptoms can take over a person's life.

What are the symptoms of anxiety?

MENTAL SYMPTOMS: These may include feeling nervous, apprehensive, panicky, on edge, or worried most or all of the time. People may also feel irritable, suffer from insomnia, be unable to concentrate, and have an exaggerated startle reflex (for example, jumping at loud noises).

PHYSICAL SYMPTOMS: These may include palpitations (a racing heart or irregular heartbeat), hyperventilation (over-breathing), feeling very hot or very cold, muscle tension, shaking or trembling, dizziness, faintness, dry mouth, problems swallowing, indigestion, and diarrhoea.

Are there different types of anxiety?

When anxiety becomes a problem that affects people's daily functioning, they may be suffering from an anxiety disorder. Some of the most common anxiety disorders are listed below (see separate factsheet for obsessive compulsive disorder):

GENERALISED ANXIETY DISORDER: GAD is the most common type of anxiety disorder, characterised by wide-ranging and excessive anxiety and worry that is difficult or impossible to control and causes significant distress and disruption in everyday life. This anxiety may apply to specific areas of life – including work, finances, relationships, and health – or be felt as more of a 'free-floating' dread, not attached to any one thing. People with GAD often have very negative thinking patterns and always believe that the worst will happen ('catastrophising').

PANIC DISORDER: Panic *attacks* are sudden episodes of intense anxiety, fear, and distress, usually lasting 5–20 minutes. Physical symptoms include palpitations, sweating, shaking, nausea, chest pain, dizziness, feeling hot or cold, shortness of breath, and feeling detached from the situation or oneself. During a panic attack people often fear that they are going to lose control, 'go crazy', or drop dead. (This is not the case: although panic attacks can be terrifying, they are not physically dangerous.) Panic *disorder* is diagnosed when a person has unexpected and repeated panic attacks where at least four of the above symptoms are present, followed by intense fear of having another attack, worry about what might happen as a result of an attack (such as dying), and/or avoidance of situations where panic attacks have happened before.

AGORAPHOBIA: Recurrent panic attacks, along with the fear of having another attack, and avoidance of situations in which attacks have previously occurred, may result in agoraphobia. Agoraphobia is not, as commonly thought, a fear of open spaces or an inability to leave the house *per se* (although it may involve both these things), but anxiety about being in situations or places where escape is difficult or embarrassing, or where help is unavailable. Such situations may include being in crowds, going to cinemas, restaurants or theatres, travelling on public transport, going across bridges or under tunnels, and being away from home. People with agoraphobia frequently avoid these situations or need to be accompanied by another person.

SOCIAL ANXIETY DISORDER: Also known as social phobia, sufferers become extremely anxious about what other people – particularly strangers – might think of them and worry that they are being judged. They fear being the centre of attention, worrying that others will notice them behaving oddly or in an anxious way, and often think that they are weak, stupid, or crazy. Social anxiety may sometimes be dismissed as extreme shyness, but for sufferers it may lead to drastic restrictions on, and distress in, their lives. They may, for example, avoid – or experience extreme anxiety during – social activities such as eating in front of other people, going to parties, having guests in the home, and work-related activities.

POST-TRAUMATIC STRESS DISORDER: PTSD may develop after exposure to a traumatic event, such as when a person has experienced or witnessed a situation involving actual or threatened death, serious injury, or sexual violence. Learning about events that involve such trauma (for example, the death of a loved one) may also trigger the condition. PTSD may manifest, for example, in soldiers who have been in combat, victims of violent crime such as rape, families of murder victims, and those caught up in natural disasters. Symptoms may include feelings of fear, horror, helplessness, flashbacks, panic attacks, nightmares, increased emotional arousal, and avoidance of feelings or situations that trigger memories of the event.

SPECIFIC PHOBIAS: People may also develop what are also known as 'simple phobias', relating to a particular object, event or situation, exposure to which may trigger excessive fear, anxiety, and panic. Some of the most common specific phobias include those relating to animals (such as dogs, spiders, or snakes), enclosed spaces, heights, blood, flying, or going to the dentist. These situations are usually avoided.

How common is anxiety?

It is thought that around 10 per cent of the general population suffer from anxiety of some description and the same amount will experience the occasional panic attack. Research suggests that 3–5 per cent suffer from GAD, 3 per cent from a specific phobia, and 1–2 per cent from panic disorder. Up to 30 per cent of people who experience a traumatic event go on to develop PTSD.

Are certain types of people more prone to developing anxiety?

Anxiety disorders are more common in women than men and are highest in people aged twenty-five to thirty-four, usually declining with age.

Why do people suffer from anxiety?

It is thought that a combination of factors causes anxiety disorders:

GENES: Research shows a strong genetic factor in some anxiety disorders. For example, nearly one in five people with panic disorder has close relatives with the condition.

ENVIRONMENT AND LIFE EXPERIENCES: Anxiety disorders may be triggered by learned behaviours (such as observing parents with anxiety problems), traumatic experiences in childhood (such as sexual or physical abuse, or poor parenting), and/or may come about from stressful events later in life (such as divorce or bereavement).

BODY CHEMISTRY: An imbalance of neurotransmitters in the brain – including serotonin, noradrenaline and gamma-aminobutyric acid – may also be involved in the development of anxiety disorders.

LIFESTYLE: Poor diet, too much caffeine, recreational drugs (such as cocaine, cannabis, and amphetamines), and stress can also cause, mirror, or exacerbate anxiety.

MEDICAL CONDITIONS AND MEDICATIONS: Some physical diseases (such as thyroid or heart problems) can cause anxiety, as well as hormone imbalances (which may occur premenstrually or in menopause). Commonly used drugs such as tobacco, and withdrawal from alcohol, narcotics, and prescription medications (such as antidepressants), may also trigger anxiety symptoms.

What is the treatment for anxiety disorders?

Most anxiety disorders are best treated by a combination of techniques:

SELF-HELP MEASURES: Relaxation techniques, breathing exercises, and meditation can be beneficial in treating anxiety. Sufferers may also find reading self-help materials and books, and joining self-help groups (one-to-one or online), helpful.

ALTERNATIVE AND COMPLIMENTARY THERAPIES: Hypnotherapy, acupuncture, and homeopathy may be effective in some cases of anxiety. The homeopathic remedy Aconite may be particularly helpful in treating anxiety and panic attacks. Some people also take herbs such as *Valeriana officinalis* (valerian), *Matricaria recutitat* (German chamomile), and *Melissa officinalis* (lemon balm) to relieve symptoms, although these may interact with prescription medications.

TALKING THERAPY: Although counselling, psychotherapy, behavioural therapy (BT), and cognitive behavioural therapy (CBT) can all be used to treat anxiety disorders, CBT and/ or BT are currently the most commonly used approaches in the UK. In BT – usually used for specific phobias – systematic desensitisation (gradual exposure) or flooding (total immersion) to whatever it is that the person fears has been found to be effective. In CBT, often used for GAD, current thinking patterns – which are usually negative, illogical, or false – are identified and replaced with more positive, logical, and realistic ones.

MEDICATION: Drugs for anxiety disorders include benzodiaze-pines ('tranquillisers'), antidepressants (such as selective serotonin reuptake inhibitors [SSRIs], tricyclics, and monoamine oxidase inhibitors [MAOIs]), beta-blockers, pregabalin, and buspirone. SSRIs are considered the first line of treatment; benzodiaze-pines are usually used for short courses only, although they may be appropriate for long-term use in particularly severe cases.

What are the risks associated with having an anxiety disorder?

Anxiety disorders can seriously affect the quality of people's lives and what they are able to do. Over a prolonged period, anxiety may also cause physical problems such as digestive issues, lower immunity, high blood pressure, and an increased risk of heart attacks and strokes. Excessive or ongoing anxiety may also lead to depression and self-medication with drugs or alcohol.

Who can I contact if I think I have an anxiety disorder?

Your first point of contact should be your GP who may per-form an examination to rule out any physical causes for the anxiety and then, if a diagnosis of anxiety is made, refer you for a course of therapy and/or prescribe medication. You may also be referred to a community mental health team (CMHT). In addition, the below organisations may be able to offer help, support, and advice:

Anxiety UK
Tel: 08444 775 774
Web: www.anxietyuk.org.uk

Anxiety Alliance
Tel: 0845 296 7877
Web: www.anxiety-alliance.org.uk

No Panic
Tel: 0800 138 8889
Web: www.nopanic.org.uk

TOP (Triumph Over Phobia)
Tel: 0845 600 9601
Web: www.topuk.org

Please see the 'Useful contacts and links' pages for more resources and organisations that may be able to help, including national mental health charities such as Mind, Sane, and Rethink.

Obsessive compulsive disorder (OCD)

What is OCD?

OCD is a type of anxiety disorder that has two key features to it: obsessions and compulsions. Obsessions are recurring, intrusive, and unwelcome thoughts, beliefs, urges, ideas, and impulses that come into the mind and cause distress and anxiety. Compulsions are repetitive behaviours and activities that the sufferer feels they have to perform to relieve the obsessive thoughts and ease the anxiety.

What are the symptoms of OCD?

OBSESSIONS: The most common obsessions in OCD are fear of contamination (such as contact with germs); excessive doubt (such as whether the door is locked); thoughts of aggression (such as doing somebody harm); fear that the person themself or someone they love may come to harm (from disease or some 'higher power'); and 'forbidden' sexual or religious thoughts.

COMPULSIONS: The most common compulsions in OCD are washing or cleaning (such as hand-washing or house-cleaning); checking (making sure the gas is off or reading through letters/ emails for mistakes); repetition of actions (such as switching a light on and off a certain number of times); ordering (such as spending a long time arranging clothes in a wardrobe); mental compulsions (such as praying, mentally repeating a phrase, or counting); and hoarding (such as keeping broken items).

Are there different types of OCD?

OCD: For a formal diagnosis of OCD, a person must be suffering from obsessions and/or compulsions that take up more than an hour of their time every day and cause distress and problems functioning in everyday life. They must also recognise that their thoughts and behaviours are irrational and take no pleasure from them.

'PURE-O': In this type of OCD obvious compulsions are absent. In these cases, sufferers may perform more hidden mental rituals or try to avoid situations that trigger obsessional thoughts (such as keeping away from places they think are dirty).

OBSESSIVE–COMPULSIVE PERSONALITY DISORDER: In OCPD the characteristics of the disorder are compatible with the person's personality (such as being a perfectionist) and the sufferer will deny that there is anything wrong, seeing their actions as rational.

How common is OCD?

It is thought that 1–3 per cent of the general population suffer from OCD.

Are certain people more likely to develop OCD?

Although it can affect people of all ages, and men and women equally, OCD usually starts before the age of 25, beginning in early adulthood for women and teenage years for men. People with OCD have also been found to have certain personality traits, including an overly developed sense of responsibility, attention to detail and planning, above average-intelligence, and avoidance of taking risks.

Why do people get OCD?

There may be several factors involved in the development of OCD:

GENES: OCD is often found to run in families. People with OCD are around four times more likely to have a family member suffering from it, in comparison with other people.

ENVIRONMENT AND LIFE EXPERIENCES: Children may learn obsessive compulsive behaviours from observing their parents. Traumatic or distressing experiences, often in childhood, may also trigger OCD, the obsessions and compulsions being used as a way of coping with anxiety.

BODY CHEMISTRY: People with OCD may have abnormalities with the neurotransmitters serotonin and dopamine.

What is the treatment for OCD?

TALKING THERAPY: Cognitive behavioural therapy (CBT) or behavioural therapy (BT) are usually recommended for OCD. Exposure and response prevention (ERP), where the sufferer is exposed to what they most fear and then attempts not to compensate with compulsive behaviours, has also been found to be particularly effective.

MEDICATION: Antidepressants, in the form of selective seroto-nin reuptake inhibitors (SSRIs), are usually the first choice of medication, sometimes along with atypical antipsychotics.

What is the prognosis for people with OCD?

It is estimated that, without treatment, people with OCD may still suffer from symptoms after thirty years. However, properly treated, the prognosis for OCD is good. Over half of people on medication improve, although symptoms may return after stopping taking the medication. The best results come from a combination of medication and ERP (or ERP alone), with around three-quarters of people who complete between ten and twenty sessions improving significantly.

What are the risks associated with OCD?

Aside from a poorer quality of life and daily distress, people with OCD are more likely to suffer from other mental health disorders, particularly panic attacks and depression. Substance abuse, sleep disturbances, tics, body dysmorphic disorder, and extreme grooming habits (such as skin picking, nail biting, and hair pulling) are also more common in people with OCD. It is estimated that more than half of people suffering from OCD have suicidal tendencies.

Who can I contact for help if I think I have OCD?

Your first point of contact should be your GP, who may pre-scribe you medication and/or refer you for therapy, depending on how severe your disorder is. In addition, the below organ-isations may be able to offer help, support, and advice:

OCD Action
Tel: 0845 390 6232
Web: www.ocdaction.org.uk

OCD-UK
Tel: 0845 120 3778
Web: www.ocduk.org

Anxiety UK
Tel: 08444 775 774
Web: www.anxietyuk.org.uk

TOP (Triumph Over Phobia)
Tel: 0845 600 9601
Web: www.topuk.org

Please see the 'Useful contacts and links' pages for more resources and organisations which may be able to help, including national mental health charities such as Mind, Sane, and Rethink.

Eating disorders: bulimia and anorexia

Eating disorders

We all have different eating habits and make personal choices about what we eat, whether that's choosing to become a vegetarian, eliminating certain foods – such as wheat or dairy – from our diet, or simply trying to eat in a healthier way. However, people whose eating choices are determined by the fear of putting on weight may have an eating disorder. In these people, avoiding calorie intake or trying to get rid of already consumed calories may become an obsession. Anorexia nervosa and bulimia nervosa are the most common eating disorders and, although they are separate conditions, often overlap.

What is bulimia?

Bulimia is an eating disorder characterised by eating large amounts of food all in one go (binge-eating) and then attempting to 'make up for it' by getting rid of the food by vomiting or using laxatives (known as 'purging'), fasting, or exercising.

What are the symptoms of bulimia?

People with bulimia usually have a distorted perception of their body shape or weight and often dislike how they look. They may crave certain foods, think about eating all the time, and have uncontrollable urges to eat large amounts. These feelings manifest in binge-eating, often over a short space of time and in secret, with sufferers often feeling out of control and disconnected from reality when binging. These episodes are then followed by vomiting, the use of laxatives, diuretics and enemas (purging), and/or fasting, diet pills, and excessive exercise. Those with bulimia may also suffer from mood swings, anxiety, depression, and have feelings of shame, guilt, and low self-esteem. People with bulimia are often of a normal weight, so it can be hard to diagnose.

Are there different types of bulimia?

PURGING BULIMIA: Those with purging bulimia binge-eat and then vomit or use laxatives, diuretics, or enemas to rid their body of the food eaten.

NON-PURGING BULIMIA: Those with non-purging bulimia – which accounts for less than 10 per cent of cases – fast or excessively exercise to get rid of the calories consumed.

How common is bulimia?

Recent research has found that up to 6.4 per cent of adults in England have symptoms of an eating disorder, with 40 per cent of those being bulimic, 10 per cent anorexic, and the rest suffering from an Eating Disorder Not Otherwise Specified (EDNOS).

Are certain types of people more likely to develop bulimia?

It is thought that women are around ten times more likely than men to suffer from bulimia, with white middle-class females being at the highest risk of developing the disorder, which usually begins between the ages of seventeen and twenty-five. Bulimia has also been found to be more common in Western nations and in those who live in urban, rather than rural, areas. Sufferers often share certain personality traits, including: perfectionism, competitiveness, low self-esteem, feelings of inferiority, difficulty in managing emotions, compulsive or obsessional behaviour, and a lack of confidence.

Why do people get bulimia?

Multiple factors are thought to contribute to the development of bulimia:

GENES: A genetic predisposition has been implicated in bulimia, as those with close family members who have suffered from the condition are more likely to suffer from it themselves.

ENVIRONMENT AND LIFE EXPERIENCES: Experiences such as childhood sexual abuse and/or neglect, and a history of family substance misuse, alcoholism, depression, and anxiety have been found to be more common in those with bulimia.

Negative or obsessional parental attitudes towards food, eating, weight, and body shape may also play a role.

BODY CHEMISTRY: Abnormal levels of neurotransmitters such as serotonin and/or of hormones such as cortisol may also contribute to the development of bulimia.

SOCIETAL/CULTURAL TRENDS: The current Western trend for slenderness, propagated by the media and the fashion industry, has also recently been implicated in the development of bulimia, where thin female 'role models' such as actresses, singers, and models are seen as images to aspire to.

What is the treatment for bulimia?

SELF-HELP MEASURES: Self-help books or guided self-help have been found to be useful initial treatments for bulimia, and sufferers may also benefit from practising relaxation techniques.

TALKING THERAPY: A range of talking therapies has been found to be helpful in the treatment of bulimia, including behaviour therapy (BT), counselling, psychotherapy, group therapy, and family therapy. However, cognitive behavioural therapy (CBT) is currently the most popular therapy for bulimia, which typically involves encouraging patients to keep food diaries of what they eat and when, noting episodes of binging and purging; educating them about nutrition and healthy eating patterns; challenging distorted thought patterns and beliefs surrounding body image, weight, food, and self-image; and focusing on strategies to prevent future relapse.

MEDICATION: Antidepressants, usually in the form of selective serotonin reuptake inhibitors (SSRIs), and specifically fluoxetine (Prozac), may also be used in some cases.

What is the prognosis for people with bulimia?

When treated with CBT, around 40–60 per cent of people with bulimia stop their cycles of binge-eating and purging. Among people treated with SSRIs alone, around 30 per cent show an improvement. Up to 70 per cent of people benefit from a combined approach.

What are the risks associated with bulimia?

Health problems that may result from bulimia include a sore throat, tooth decay, constipation, IBS, a stretched colon, bad breath, swollen glands, loss of libido, bad skin, hair loss, lethargy, vitamin and mineral deficiencies, irregular periods, epilepsy, and heart problems. People with bulimia are also more vulnerable to anxiety and depression and more likely to engage in other extreme or impulsive behaviours such as inappropriate sexual encounters, shoplifting, substance misuse, self-harm, and overspending.

What is anorexia?

Anorexia is a type of eating disorder in which sufferers have a distorted view of their body image and are terrified of gaining weight, refusing to keep to a normal body weight and being at least 15 per cent below the average healthy weight for their size. They severely restrict their food intake and/or starve themselves in order to lose weight and often still think that they are fat even when they are life-threateningly thin.

What are the symptoms of anorexia?

People suffering from anorexia may restrict their calorie intake, starve themselves, vomit after eating, and/or use laxatives and diuretics. They may also smoke or chew gum to curb hunger.

Even though their weight loss is obvious, and usually occurs over a short time frame, they often try to convince others that they do not have a problem. In order to avoid eating any, or much, food, they may claim to have already eaten, avoid socialising where there is food, deny being hungry, hide food, pick at small amounts on their plate, or pile their plate high with salad or vegetables. They may privately research weight loss methods, obsess about the calories and fat contained in different foods, and constantly weigh themselves and examine their appearance. As they are always hungry they may be preoccupied with the thought of food and often buy and cook it for others. They may also display other obsessive behaviours such as excessive cleaning and washing.

Are there different types of anorexia?

RESTRICTING TYPE: In these cases, sufferers essentially starve themselves by severely restricting what they eat.

BINGE-EATING/PURGING TYPE: In these cases, sufferers regularly overeat and then purge.

How common is anorexia?

It is thought that up to 6.4 per cent of adults in England have symptoms of an eating disorder, with 10 per cent of those being anorexic, 40 per cent being bulimic, and the rest suffering from an Eating Disorder Not Otherwise Specified (EDNOS).

Are certain types of people more likely to develop anorexia?

Research has found that anorexia is most common in white middle-class teenage girls in Western countries. People with anorexia have also been found to share certain personality traits, often being perfectionists and high-achievers who have very high expectations of themselves and hate making mistakes. Underneath this they frequently have low self-esteem, lack self-confidence, fear rejection and failure, feel inadequate and are eager to please.

Why do people get anorexia?

It is thought that a number of factors can contribute to the development of anorexia:

GENES: Anorexia is thought to have a strong genetic link. Those with close family members with anorexia are around 30 per cent more likely to develop the condition.

ENVIRONMENT AND LIFE EXPERIENCES: Those with anorexia often come from families with parents who have strict rules, avoid showing emotions or having confrontations, and make negative comments about weight and/or frequently diet. Distressing life events such as leaving home, bereavement, divorce, and illnesses may also be contributing factors.

PSYCHOLOGICAL FACTORS: People with anorexia may often feel out of control in their lives, or an aspect of their lives, and use the condition as a way to regain control. They may also suffer from a large amount of internalised anger and rage that they are unable to express.

SOCIETAL FACTORS: Societies and cultures that idealise thinness are more likely to have higher rates of anorexia.

What is the treatment for anorexia?

TALKING THERAPIES: Counselling, cognitive behavioural therapy (CBT), group therapy, and family therapy are all commonly employed. Advice on nutrition and how to gain weight safely (such as eating small amounts of food regularly) are also given.

MEDICATION: Medication may also sometimes be used, usually in the form of selective serotonin reuptake inhibitors (SSRIs) or Olanzapine, an atypical antipsychotic.

HOSPITALISATION: If the sufferer is dangerously underweight then they may need to go to a hospital or clinic which will run a series of physical health checks, help the sufferer to start eating normally again, monitor their weight gain, and control their anxiety about this. In rare cases, when the condition is severe and the sufferer refuses help, they may be detained under the Mental Health Act ('sectioned').

What is the prognosis for people with anorexia?

Those suffering from anorexia are usually ill for an average of 5–7 years and over half of those recover from the condition. However, people with anorexia have the highest death rate of all mental illnesses, with around one in five of those whose condition is severe enough for hospitalisation dying. The death rate is much lower in people who have ongoing support and medical help.

What are the risks associated with anorexia?

Anorexia is associated with numerous physical problems, from the mild to the life-threatening. Those with anorexia may suffer from constipation, abdominal pain, bloating, dizziness, fainting, feeling cold, poor circulation, dry/rough/mottled skin, sleep disruption, increased body hair, dehydration, electrolyte imbalances, epilepsy, anaemia, infections, low blood pressure, difficulty concentrating, brittle bones (which can lead to osteoporosis), organ damage, and heart problems, which may be fatal. Girls and women may also stop having their periods, leading to infertility.

Who can I contact for help if I think I have bulimia or anorexia?

Your first point of contact should be your GP, who may recommend a range of treatment options depending on the severity of your condition, from self-help measures, a referral for CBT or other therapy, dietary advice, and medication. If you have bulimia it is very unlikely that you will need to be hospitalised; however, if you suffer from anorexia and are dangerously underweight then hospitalisation may be necessary. In addition, the below organisations may be able to offer help, support, and advice:

Beat (Beating Eating Disorders)
Tel: 0845 634 1414 (adult helpline)
Tel: 0845 634 7650 (youthline)
Web: www.b-eat.co.uk

Anorexia and Bulimia Care (ABC)
Tel: 030 00 11 12 13
Web: www.anorexiabulimiacare.org.uk

MGEDT (Men Get Eating Disorders Too)
Web: http://mengetedstoo.co.uk

Please see the 'Useful contacts and links' pages for more resources and organisations which may be able to help, including national mental health charities such as Mind, Sane, and Rethink.

Body dysmorphic disorder (BDD)

What is BDD?

People with BDD are excessively concerned about their body image, with sufferers often becoming obsessed over perceived 'imperfections' on their body or face. They frequently think that such 'flaws' make them ugly or disgusting, which has lead to the disorder sometimes being referred to as 'Imagined Ugliness Syndrome'.

What are the symptoms of BDD?

People with BDD may spend hours every day preoccupied by their perceived defect(s), most frequently involving the nose, eyes, skin, lips, mouth, chin, jaw, and general build. Sufferers, for example, may think that their body parts are the wrong shape or size; they may be concerned over wrinkles or acne; and may obsess over hair loss or receding. They may constantly look in mirrors (or avoid their reflection), examine the part of themselves they are unhappy with, compare themselves to others, and seek reassurance about how they look. As they often see themselves as ugly or abnormal (and think others must too) they may try to hide their 'defect(s)' with make-up, hats, clothing, and the avoidance of bright lights. A diagnosis of BDD is made when these symptoms cause significant distress or disrupt daily life.

How common is BDD?

It is difficult to estimate how common BDD is as sufferers usually believe that they have an actual physical problem so do not
seek psychological help. However, it is thought that 1–5 per
cent of the population may be affected, with 12–15 per cent of
people seen by dermatologists and cosmetic surgeons suffering
from BDD.

Are certain types of people more prone to developing BDD?

BDD usually starts early in life, when children or adolescents
are very sensitive about how they look, although it can also
begin in adulthood. Well-educated people who work in an
artistic field may also be particularly prone to BDD.

Why do people get BDD?

There has been little research into why people develop BDD.
However, like most mental illnesses, there may be genetic,
environmental, and psychological factors involved. It is thought
that bullying, teasing, and abuse in childhood, resulting in low
self-esteem, may play a particular role in the development of
BDD.

What is the treatment for BDD?

Many people with BDD consult cosmetic practitioners, rather
than seeking psychological help, as they believe that correcting
the 'defect' will make them happy. However, cosmetic procedures do not generally work, as the person often doesn't like
the results or just begins to obsess about another body part.

In extreme cases, sufferers may undergo repeated cosmetic procedures.

TALKING THERAPIES: When psychological help is sought, sufferers are usually offered self-help literature and cognitive behavioural therapy (CBT). During CBT the sufferer may be encouraged to challenge their negative thoughts and beliefs about their body image; learn how to curb obsessive rituals and behaviours (such as constantly looking in the mirror); and be exposed to situations that make them anxious (such as not hiding the perceived flaw).

MEDICATION: Antidepressants, usually selective serotonin reuptake inhibitors (SSRIs) – and specifically fluoxetine (Prozac) – may also be prescribed.

What is the prognosis for people with BDD?

Talking therapy and/or medication can often improve the quality of life for BDD sufferers, although for some the condition may be chronic.

What are the risks associated with BDD?

BDD may affect many aspects of sufferers' lives – including their education, social life, and work – as they think that other people are judging how they look, which may lead to unemployment and isolation (to the extent that some people become housebound). People with BDD also frequently suffer from other mental health conditions, such as depression, OCD, and/or social anxiety, and may have substance abuse problems. Some people with BDD may self-mutilate – attempting cosmetic or corrective procedures on themselves – and also have suicidal thoughts or attempt suicide.

Who can I contact for help if I think I have BDD?

Your first point of contact should be your GP who may offer you self-help materials, refer you for CBT, and/or prescribe an antidepressant. They may also be able to refer you to a support group (online or in person) where you can share experiences with other people with BDD. If more treatment is needed then the local community mental health team (CMHT) can assess you and may refer you to a specialist BDD clinic, although unfortunately waiting times are frequently long. In addition, the below organisations may be able to offer help, support, and advice:

The BDD Foundation
Web: www.thebddfoundation.com/index.htm

OCD Action
Tel: 0845 390 6232
Web: www.ocdaction.org.uk

OCD-UK
Tel: 0845 120 3778
Web: www.ocduk.org

Anxiety UK
Tel: 08444 775 774
Web: www.anxietyuk.org.uk

Please see the 'Useful contacts and links' pages for more resources and organisations which may be able to help, including national mental health charities such as Mind, Sane, and Rethink.

Glossary of terms

Anticonvulsants are medications used primarily to treat epilepsy, which work by suppressing the excessive firing of neurons in the brain that trigger seizures. However, some anticonvulsants may also be used to treat mental health conditions. For example, sodium valporate may be used as a mood stabiliser for people with bipolar disorder, and pregabalin may be prescribed for generalised anxiety disorder.

Antidepressants are psychoactive drugs used for the treatment of depression and other mental health conditions. They include different classes of medication, such as selective serotonin reuptake inhibitors (SSRIs), serotonin–norepinephrine reuptake inhibitors (SNRIs), tricyclic antidepressants, and monoamine oxidase inhibitors (MAOIs). They work by increasing the levels of certain neurotransmitters in the brain, such as serotonin and norepinephrine, which improve mood.

Antipsychotics or neuroleptics are psychoactive drugs used mainly to treat psychotic conditions such as schizophrenia. However, antipsychotics may also be used in the treatment of other mental health disorders, such as bipolar disorder, severe anxiety, and depression. There are two classes of antipsychotic drug: typical (e.g. chlorpromazine) and atypical (e.g. quetiapine). While both work by blocking the effects of dopamine, atypical antipsychotics also affect serotonin.

Assertive outreach teams work with people who are experiencing the most severe kinds of mental illness who are unable to engage with, or who have lost touch with, mainstream services.

Behavioural therapy (BT) is based on the premise that behaviour is learnt and, therefore, can be unlearnt. As a type of therapy, it may include systematic desensitisation, aversion therapy, and flooding. Flooding, for example, is a technique that may be used to overcome phobias, involving exposing the patient to their feared object or situation until their fear subsides. The therapist may help the patient during this process by using relaxation techniques.

Benzodiazepines (BZDs, 'benzos', or 'tranquillisers') are psychoactive drugs that work by enhancing the chemical GABA in the brain, producing calming effects. They reduce anxiety, promote sleep, relax muscles, have anticonvulsant properties, and are sedating. Although they are very effective for anxiety states, they are usually only used as a short-term treatment due to their addictive qualities. Diazepam (Valium) is an example of a benzodiazepine.

Beta-blockers are medications that block the release of adrenaline and noradrenaline in various parts of the body. Although they are usually used to treat heart problems and high blood pressure, they may also sometimes be used to treat the physical symptoms of anxiety, such as palpitations and shaking. However, they do not help the mental symptoms of anxiety, such as feelings of worry or dread.

Cognitive behavioural therapy (CBT) is a type of talking therapy that focuses on the here and now rather than the past. It attempts to change the way a person thinks (their cognitions) and how they respond to these thoughts (their behaviour). It may, for example, involve identifying and challenging negative and unhelpful thought patterns and replacing them with positive ones, leading to beneficial behavioural change. It is frequently used to treat depression, anxiety, and eating disorders.

Community mental health teams (CMHT) are made up of different types of professionals – such as psychiatrists, social workers, community psychiatric nurses, and support workers – who work together to give care to people with mental illness.

Cortisol is a steroid hormone released by the adrenal gland. It is sometimes known as a 'stress' hormone as it is released into the bloodstream in response to stress.

Crisis services are services available at short notice to support people through an acute mental health episode. Available on the NHS or through charities, such services can be in the form of telephone helplines, acute inpatient wards in hospitals, and/ or crisis resolution and home treatment (CRHT) teams.

Delusions are irrational and illogical beliefs that may occur in certain mental illnesses, such as schizophrenia. Somebody experiencing delusions may think, for example, that their phone is a mind-control device or that they are being followed or monitored by a law enforcement agency.

Dopamine is a neurotransmitter produced in the brain which is often known as a 'feel good' chemical as it controls the brain's reward and pleasure centres.

Early intervention services (EIS) are local teams – made up of experts such as psychiatrists, psychologists, social workers, support workers, and occupational therapists – who give help and support to people who have recently experienced their first psychotic episode.

Electroconvulsive therapy (ECT) involves having an electrical current passed through the brain while under general anaesthetic. It is usually only used in cases of severe clinical depression that have not responded to other treatment. It is unclear exactly how ECT works but it can be very effective in the short term, although it doesn't seem to stop depression coming back in the future.

Exposure and response prevention (ERP) is a type of therapy, used particularly in anxiety disorders such as phobias and OCD. Used in the treatment of OCD, it involves a patient, guided by their therapist, being exposed to what they most fear, without then compensating with compulsive behaviours. For example, a person with a fear of germs might be encouraged to gradually build up to touching a toilet seat without washing their hands afterwards. If the patient is able to complete the course of therapy it has been found to be very effective.

Gamma-aminobutyric acid (GABA) is a neurotransmitter that helps to regulate over-excitement of the nervous system. Drugs that enhance GABA – such as benzodiazapines – have a calming effect.

Hallucinations can affect all of the senses and may involve hearing, seeing, smelling, tasting, or feeling things that aren't actually there. For example, people experiencing hallucinations may hear voices in their head or feel as if there are insects crawling on their skin. Hallucinations may be symptoms of a mental illness such as schizophrenia or may be induced by drugs, alcohol, or a physical illness (such as infection).

Interpersonal therapy (IPT) is a type of therapeutic approach that views psychological symptoms as being a response to current problems and conflicts in the relationships in a person's life. As a therapy, it is structured and time-limited, usually performed over a course of between eight and sixteen sessions.

Monoamine oxidase inhibitors (MAOIs) are an older form of antidepressant drug that are usually only used today when other medications haven't worked. They have to be used with care as they can interact dangerously with foods that contain high levels of tyramine, such as aged cheeses, fermented foods, liver, alcohol, yeast, and some meats. Eating such foods while taking MAOIs may result in seriously high blood pressure and, in severe cases, can be fatal.

Neurotransmitters are chemical substances that transmit signals between nerve cells in the brain.

Norepinephrine/noradrenaline is a neurotransmitter and hormone. It is commonly known as a 'stress hormone' or 'fight or flight chemical' as it underpins the body's 'fight or flight' response, speeding up the heart rate, raising blood pressure, narrowing blood vessels in non-essential organs, and dilating pupils.

Psychiatrists are medical doctors who go on to specialise in the diagnosis and treatment of mental health disorders. Unlike psychologists, they are able to prescribe medication.

Psychoanalysis is a type of psychotherapy, initially developed by Sigmund Freud. Its underlying premise is that early childhood experiences provide unconscious patterns which affect a person's psychological well-being and functioning into adulthood. In psychoanalysis such patterns are brought back into conscious awareness so that a patient can understand what is creating their mental distress.

Psychologists are specialists in human behaviour. Clinical or counselling psychologists are trained to work with people with mental health conditions. They may work in various settings, such as hospitals, health centres, or privately.

Psychosis is a general term that describes mental states where people are out of touch with reality. Psychotic symptoms may include hallucinations, delusions, and muddled, disordered, and jumbled thinking. Psychosis is not a mental health disorder in itself but may be a symptom of other disorders, such as schizophrenia or bipolar I disorder. Psychotic symptoms may also be brought on by traumatic events or by some physical illnesses (such as infections).

Psychosomatic symptoms or somatisation is the tendency to experience and express psychological distress in the form of physical symptoms such as chest pain, palpitations, headaches, nausea, insomnia, dizziness, and fatigue.

Psychosurgery/neurosurgery involves using brain surgery to treat mental illness, by destroying or removing a small piece of the brain. Today, psychosurgery is very rarely used in the UK and can only be carried out with the patient's permission.

Psychotherapy is an umbrella term that generally refers to the process of talking therapy conducted by a trained therapist with a patient experiencing psychological distress. The treatment aims to increase the patient's sense of well-being and improve their mental health. Psychotherapy may also encompass non-talking therapies such as art, drama, or music therapy.

Schizophrenia is a mental illness that affects the way that a person thinks, feels, and behaves. The symptoms of schizophrenia are often classed as 'positive' and 'negative'. Positive symptoms include hallucinations, delusions, and jumbled thinking ('not thinking straight'). Negative symptoms may include memory problems, an inability to concentrate, becoming isolated, problems communicating with other people, and loss of interest in usual activities.

Sectioning, or being sectioned, is when a person is detained at a hospital under the Mental Health Act, whether or not they agree to it. In order to be sectioned someone must be suffering from a mental health condition that needs treatment or assessment in hospital, in order to protect their own safety or other people's safety.

Selective serotonin reuptake inhibitors (SSRIs) are antidepressant medications, used to treat a variety of mental illnesses, that are thought to work by increasing the levels of serotonin in the brain. They are usually now used instead of the older-style antidepressants as they have fewer side effects. SSRIs can take up to four weeks to work and patients usually start on a small dose, which is then gradually increased, in order to minimise side effects. Similarly, when discontinuing treatment, the medication should be gradually reduced. Some people may have to try several different SSRIs before they find one that works for them. Fluoxetine (Prozac) is an example of an SSRI.

Serotonin is a neurotransmitter that regulates mood. It is thought that those with low levels of serotonin may be prone to depression.

Tricyclics are an older style of antidepressant medication that affect three neurotransmitters: serotonin, norepinephrine, and acetylcholine. They are now generally less popular than SSRIs, as their 'anticholinergic' effects can have adverse effects on the heart and circulation, and taking more than the prescribed dose can be dangerous. Examples of tricyclics include amitriptyline and imipramine.

Useful contacts and links

Mind

Infoline: 0300 123 3393
Web: www.mind.org.uk
A charity that provides advice and support to those living with mental illness.

Rethink

Helpline: 0300 5000 927
Web: www.rethink.org
A charity that provides information, services, and a voice for those affected by mental illness.

SANE

Helpline: 0845 767 8000
Email: info@sane.org.uk
Web: www.sane.org.uk
A charity that provides emotional support, information, and practical help to people suffering from mental illness.

The Samaritans

24-hour helpline: 08457 90 90 90
Email: jo@samaritans.org
Web: www.samaritans.org
A 24-hour service that provides confidential emotional support for people who are in distress or having suicidal thoughts.

Mental Health Foundation

Web: www.mentalhealth.org.uk
A charity that aims to help people live with and recover from mental illness, through research, campaigning, and pioneering practical solutions. It provides statistics and information on mental health conditions for the public.

The Mental Elf

Web: www.thementalelf.net
Up-to-date information on mental health research, policy, and guidance.

NHS Choices

Web: www.nhs.uk
National Health Service information on mental health conditions, treatments, local services, and healthy living.

British Association for Counselling and Psychotherapy (BACP)

Tel: 01455 883300
Web: www.bacp.co.uk
The largest professional body representing counselling and psychotherapy, including an accredited register where members of the public can find therapists in their area.

British Association for Behavioural and Cognitive Psychotherapies (BABCP)

Tel: 0161 705 4304
Web: www.babcp.com
An interest group for those involved in the area of behavioural and cognitive psychotherapy, providing information about CBT for the public and a register of all officially accredited CBT therapists.

Royal College of Psychiatrists

Tel: 020 7235 2351
Web: www.rcpsych.ac.uk
The professional body that is responsible for education, training, and raising standards in psychiatry. RCPsych also provides information about mental health conditions for the public.

Carers UK

Helpline: 0808 808 7777
Web: www.carersuk.org
A charity that provides help, advice, and support for anyone caring for an older, disabled, or seriously ill family member or friend.

Acknowledgements

Our thanks must go, first and foremost, to the people whose stories are featured in the preceding chapters; there would be no book without you. We have been touched and humbled by your willingness to share your most personal experiences with us and the public and by your enthusiasm for this project.

We are also immensely grateful to Andreas Campomar, and everyone else at Constable & Robinson, who saw the potential in, commissioned, and worked on, this book, as well as to those who helped put us in touch with some of the people whose stories are featured here.

So too are we indebted to Dr Richard Bowskill, both for writing the Afterword and for his sensible and thoughtful professional treatment over the past few years, and to Marilyn Finch for her therapeutic help, wisdom, patience, and behavioural experiments(!).

Many thanks also go to Rick Gekoski and Belinda Kitchin, who read, edited, and gave helpful opinions on the entire manuscript, as well as to those who read drafts of individual chapters, including Barbara Gekoski, Cathy Broome, Polly Mosley, Kate Hartshorn, Tom Heywood, Charlie Heywood, Mark Owen, and Gem Catlin. Particular thanks here go to Alison Dunn, who took the time to read the whole book and give thoughtful and constructive comments just one week before she gave birth to her beautiful daughter Caitlin.

We would also like to give a special mention to Anna's brother Bertie (Aaron), who not only read drafts of chapters but also came up with the title of the book and took the author photographs.

Lastly, we would like to say a huge 'thank you' to our family and friends − you know who you are − who have supported and helped us through some very difficult times. We love you all. And finally to Mavis, our dog, for his (yes, *his*) boundless perky energy that has cheered us up when we've needed it the most.